Accounting:
A Brief Introduction

Alastair Matchett

SOUTH-WESTERN

THOMSON LEARNING

Australia · Canada · Mexico · Singapore · Spain · United Kingdom · United States

SOUTH-WESTERN
™
THOMSON LEARNING

Accounting: A Brief Introduction, 1e

Alastair Matchett

Vice President/Editor-in-Chief:
Jack W. Calhoun

Team Leader:
Melissa S. Acuña

Acquisitions Editor:
Sharon Oblinger

Developmental Editor:
Mardell Toomey

Production Editor:
Salvatore N. Versetto

Manufacturing Coordinator:
Doug Wilke

Compositor:
Navta Associates, Inc.

Printer:
Transcontinental Printing, Inc.
Peterborough, ON

Design Project Manager:
Rick A. Moore

Internal Designer:
John Robb, JWR Design Interaction

Cover Designer:
John Robb, JWR Design Interaction

About this Book

It will help you *succeed* — Your knowledge of basic accounting skills is one of the most significant predictors of your success as a financial analyst.

It's *streamlined* — This book is not a detailed general accounting course. It focuses only on the accounting and financial skills you need to understand financial statements and analyze company performance.

It's *self-paced* — Move at your own pace. Go straight to the checkout tests if you already know the material in a section and simply want to check yourself.

How to Use this Book

If you. . .

Have little or no accounting experience. . .start here →

> **Part 1** **The basics**
> Introduction to basic accounting
> *Checkout test*

↓

Know some accounting. . . Want to review key concepts. . .start here →

> **Part 2** **Accounting for Financial Analysts**
> The accounting concepts and skills financial analysts must know and use
> *Checkout test*

↓

Already know accounting. . . start here →

> **Part 3** **Ratio Analysis**
> Key ratios and how they're used
> *Checkout test*

↓

At the end, earn the bonus on the final deal! →

> **Final Deal**
> Reviews all the material

Table of Contents

Part 2 Accounting for Financial Analysis

Introduction

Accounting Performs three Helpful Tasks

1. It **uses numbers** to **describe companies** and other entities (like governments, individuals, and non-profit organizations) **and their activities.**

2. It organizes the information into **financial statements.**

3. It **provides a standard** so you can compare the performance of different companies, or examine the same company's performance over time.

Think of Accounting as the Language of Business

Accounting helps different businesses **describe their activities consistently and clearly.** A fashion retail business and an auto parts manufacturer can both use accounting to communicate the results of their activities.

Companies in different countries use slightly different "dialects" of the accounting language. The accounting language of the United States describes some procedures slightly differently than the accounting language of the United Kingdom. For example, a British company's accounts record the purchase of another company differently than a US company's accounts do.

Accounting follows a set of agreed-upon concepts, principles, and procedures called Generally Accepted Accounting Principles **(GAAP)**. GAAP ensures that a company's financial statements present its business activities fairly.

Each country has its own set of GAAP procedures, such as US GAAP, UK GAAP and French GAAP.

Accounting represents information about an entity

Companies, individuals, organizations and governments can all be **entities.** Financial statements report information about an entity. They do not report information about the owners', customers', or employees' activities.

EXERCISE 1 ▶
*Accounting entities
(Sample Exercise)*

Accounting Entities

Apply the entity concept to the Chase Bank. Check the items you would include in Chase's financial statements.

❑ 1. One Chase shareholder owns three red Ferraris.

❑ 2. A Chase employee spent $1,000 on a flight to Argentina to meet with a client.

❑ 3. Another Chase employee recently bought a $300,000 apartment in Manhattan.

❑ 4. Toyota borrowed $200m from Chase to buy a parts supply company.

Part One:

The Basics

The Balance Sheet
1. The Parts of a Balance Sheet

The balance sheet is a snapshot . . .

Accounting organizes financial information about an entity into financial statements. One very important financial statement is the **balance sheet**.

It takes a picture of the assets a company owns at one moment in time. It also shows how those assets were **funded** (paid). The balance sheet for an entity changes each time a new transaction is recorded.

The Balance Sheet has two Lists or Sides

One list or side of the balance sheet records resources the company owns (**assets** is the correct accounting term). The other list shows you how the company funded those assets. Printed copies of the balance sheet may show the two lists side by side or one above the other.

Resources (assets)

How the resources were funded

The two sides of the balance sheet

Each side of the balance sheet contains lists of different accounts. Each account represents a particular type of asset or funding.

ASSETS: THE RESOURCES SIDE OF THE BALANCE SHEET

Assets

A person may own a house to live in, a business may own a factory to manufacture products, and a bank has cash on hand for its tellers.

Accounting refers to these resources as **assets**.

An asset must satisfy three requirements before you can record it on the balance sheet:

1. The entity must **own** it.

2. It must be **valuable** to the entity ("*provide probable future benefit*").

3. It must be acquired at a **measurable cost**.

The word from GAAP

"Assets are probable future economic benefits obtained or controlled by a particular entity."

3

EXERCISE 1 ▶
Find the Assets

The balance sheet shows the original cost of assets

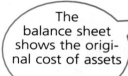

Assets   Liabilities

Recording Assets on the Balance Sheet

Which assets would General Motors record on its balance sheet?
Hint: Use the three requirements.

❑ 1. Cash

❑ 2. People

❑ 3. Trees next to the factory

❑ 4. Machinery for manufacturing cars in its factory

❑ 5. Inventories of cars ready to be sold

❑ 6. An office building that GM owns

The balance sheet lists the assets a company owns and tells you the dollar price it paid for them. Assets appear on the **left side** of the balance sheet.

THE FUNDING SIDE OF THE BALANCE SHEET

If an entity owns assets, it must have paid for them in some way. The **right side** of the balance sheet shows how a company funds the assets recorded on the left side. A company can fund assets by either **liabilities** or **equity**.

Liabilities

Liabilities record what you owe to other entities. A liability must satisfy two requirements:

1. It must be a *measurable obligation*.

2. It must be *likely to happen* ("*probable*").

The word from GAAP

"Liabilities are probable future sacrifices of economic benefit arising from present obligations of a particular entity."

> **EXAMPLE**
>
> Your company orders 500 cases of paper. The bill for $1,000 is due at the end of the month.
>
> *The unpaid bill is a liability of $1,000.*
>
> Your company borrows $100,000 from the bank.
>
> *The loan is a liability of $100,000.*
>
> Your company owes $20,000 in taxes but has not yet paid them.
>
> *The unpaid taxes are a liability of $20,000.*

Find the Liabilities

Check the liabilities GM would record on its balance sheet:

- ❑ 1. A $100m loan
- ❑ 2. Taxes of $10,000 owed to the government
- ❑ 3. $1,000 in cash in GM's bank account
- ❑ 4. The possibility that an earthquake might hit GM's Los Angeles office

Liability holders can claim your assets

Everything has a price! In return for helping your company get resources, liability holders have a claim against all your company's assets. If you don't pay your liabilities when they are due, the entity that supplied you with resources (the paper supply company, the bank, the government) can claim your assets. The liability holders have a right to make a claim on any of your assets, not just the ones they supplied.

Equity Represents the Owner's Investment

Owners of a corporation are called **shareholders**. Their investment in the company appears in the **equity section** on the **right** *(funding)* **side** of the balance sheet.

Equity has two elements:

1. *Paid-in capital*

   In return for supplying funds to the company, investors receive **shares** of stock. The funds they supplied are recorded as **paid-in-capital (PIC)** on the balance sheet.

2. *Retained earnings*

   A company's after-tax profits are available to its shareholders. The company can either pay out profits to shareholders as **dividends** or retain profits in the business.

   Profits retained in the business are recorded as **retained earnings**. A company pays dividends to shareholders out of its store of retained earnings.

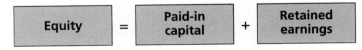

| Equity | = | Paid-in capital | + | Retained earnings |

Both paid-in capital and retained earnings help fund the assets on the left side of the balance sheet.

EXERCISE 3 ▶
CloseShave's Equity Accounts

Changes in the Equity Accounts

1. When a shareholder invests money in a business, in which account does the company record the shareholders' interest?
   ❏ Paid-in capital   ❏ Retained earnings

2. If CloseShave's shareholders supplied an additional $200m in cash to the company, which equity account would rise and which asset account would rise? *(Hint: Cash is an asset account.)*

   Assets   **Equity**

3. If CloseShave retained $900m profit in one year, which equity account would rise and by how much?

   _____ | |

Equity holders take more risk

Shareholders also have a claim against the assets of a business. However, their claim on the assets ranks after the claims of owners of liabilities *(creditors)*. If a company goes bankrupt, the owners of liabilities are first in line for the proceeds.

Because they don't have first claim on the assets, owners of equity take more **risk** than owners of liabilities.

EXERCISE 4 ▶
Equity and Risk

Liabilities, Equity, and Risk

You recently started your job as a financial analyst on Wall Street. Your vice president asks you to look at the following balance sheet:

CloseShave's Balance Sheet on December 31, 2000

Assets	$8,940m	Liabilities	$5,040m
		Equity	$3,900m
Total	**$8,940m**	**Total**	**$8,940m**

Then she asks you the following questions:

1. [   ] What if the CloseShave company went bankrupt? How much of the total assets would CloseShave's liability holders claim?

2. Whose claim would be paid first in question 1?
   ❏ Liability owners' claims   ❏ Equity owners' claims

3. Which is riskier to own, a company's ❏ equity or ❏ debt?

RESOURCES MUST EQUAL FUNDING

Total resources on one side of the balance sheet must always equal the total funding on the opposite side.

The totals on both sides of the balance sheet must be equal

If you increase or decrease only one side, you must make another **change** so that the two sides are equal again.

If you add **resources** to a company's balance sheet, you must . . .

Either subtract resources . . .

. . . or add funding

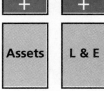

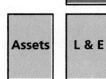

If you add **funding** to a company's balance sheet, you must . . .

Either subtract funding . . .

. . . or add resources

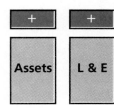

The two sides must balance

7

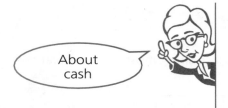

About cash

In Exercise 5, you need to know that when accounting refers to "cash," it can mean any of the following:

Bills and coins   **Checks**

Money orders   **Wire transfers**

Very liquid securities (US Treasury bills)

EXERCISE 5 ▶
The Clothing Company

Create a Balance Sheet

Imagine you own a retail clothing company. You have $340m worth of resources which you paid for by a $340m bank loan. Your balance sheet would look like this:

Balance sheet		
Total resources $340m	**=**	**Total funding** $340m

1. [_____] If you went to the bank and raised another $10m of loans, what would your total funding be?

2. [_____] The $10m loan was in the form of cash. What is the amount of your total resources now?

3. Now update your balance sheet:

Balance sheet		
Total resources [_____]	**=**	**Total funding** [_____]

Hint: Remember that your balance sheet must always balance.

Suppose you decide to reduce the amount of your bank loan by paying $30m cash back to the bank:

4. [_____] What would be your new total funding? *(Use your new balance sheet totals)*

5. [_____] What would be your new total resources? *(Use your new balance sheet totals)*

6. Now update your balance sheet.

Balance sheet

Balance sheet		
Total resources [_____]	**=**	**Total funding** [_____]

*Financial
analysis tip*

Sources and Uses of Funds

Financial analysts refer to **sources and uses of funds**. Companies spend money on assets, so they represent *uses of funds.* Liabilities and equity show where the funding comes from, so they are *sources of funds.*

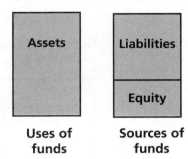

You now know . . .

■ **The balance sheet must balance.**
■ **The assets a company owns appear on the left side.**
■ **Assets are funded by liabilities and equity, which appear on the right side.**
■ **Assets must equal liabilities plus equity: A = L + E.**
■ **Financial analysts refer to sources and uses of funds.**

2. Building a Simple Balance Sheet

Balance an increase in assets by…

…increasing liabilities

…or increasing equity…

…or reducing another asset

Now you're ready to build a simple balance sheet. First, look at some examples.

EXAMPLE

Suppose Goldman Stanley *(not a real company!)* buys a car for one of its officers. The car costs $50,000. Goldman Stanley has 3 choices:

Option 1 Goldman Stanley takes out a loan to finance the car. It adds $50,000 to assets and $50,000 to liabilities.

Assets		Liabilities & Equity	
Car	$50,000	Loan	$50,000
		Paid-in capital	$0
Total	**$50,000**	**Total**	**$50,000**

Option 2 Goldman Stanley raises money from shareholders to buy the car. It adds $50,000 to assets and $50,000 to equity.

Assets		Liabilities & Equity	
Car	$50,000	Loan	$0
		Paid-in capital	$50,000
Total	**$50,000**	**Total**	**$50,000**

Option 3 Goldman Stanley uses its available cash.

Assets		Liabilities & Equity	
Cash	$100,000	Loan	$0
		Paid-in capital	$100,000
Total	**$100,000**	**Total**	**$100,000**

The cash originally came from selling stock. First Goldman Stanley issues $100,000 of stock and receives cash.

Now Goldman Stanley uses some of its cash to buy the car. Remember the balance sheet must still balance. Goldman Stanley's cash balance falls by $50,000 but it adds a new asset, the $50,000 car.

Assets		Liabilities & Equity	
Cash	$50,000	Loan	$0
Car	$50,000	Paid-in capital	$100,000
Total	**$100,000**	**Total**	**$100,000**

Goldman Stanley reduces one asset and adds a new asset, adjusting only one side of the balance sheet.

EXERCISE 6 ▶
Gregs rental agency Part 1

Greg's Rental Agency, part 1

Greg sets up a rental agency for summer houses in the Hamptons (a resort area outside New York City, popular with investment bankers). You have volunteered to keep his accounts for him.

Add the appropriate accounts to your balance sheet for each transaction below. Keep a running total from balance sheet to balance sheet.

1. Greg invests $1,000 cash as paid-in capital to set up the company.

Balance sheet	
Assets	**Liabilities**
Cash _____	_____
	Equity
	PIC _____
Total assets _____	**Total L&E** _____

2. Greg gets a $1,000 loan from the bank and receives cash.

Balance sheet	
Assets	**Liabilities**
Cash _____	Loan _____
	Equity
	PIC _____
Total assets _____	**Total L&E** _____

continued on next page

Greg's Rental Agency, part 1, continued

3. Greg buys a beach hut for an office for $500. He pays cash.

Balance sheet			
Assets		**Liabilities**	
Cash	_____	Loan	_____
Beach hut	_____	**Equity**	
		PIC	_____
Total assets	_____	**Total L&E**	_____

4. Greg buys a car for $200 with a new bank loan.

Balance sheet			
Assets		**Liabilities**	
Cash	_____	Loans	_____
Beach hut	_____	**Equity**	
Car	_____	PIC	_____
Total assets	_____	**Total L&E**	_____

5. Greg buys stationery and other office incidentals for $100 cash.

Balance sheet			
Assets		**Liabilities**	
Cash	_____	Loans	_____
Beach hut	_____		
Car	_____	**Equity**	
Ofc. supplies	_____	PIC	_____
Total assets	_____	**Total L&E**	_____

6. Greg decides the car is no use on the beach. He sells the car for $200 and pays back the $200 bank loan. He also purchases a bicycle for $50 cash.

Balance sheet			
Assets		**Liabilities**	
Cash	_____	Loan	_____
Beach hut	_____		
Bicycle	_____	**Equity**	
Ofc. supplies	_____	PIC	_____
Total assets	_____	**Total L&E**	_____

Making multiple entries for one transaction

In the rental agency exercise, you made two changes to the balance sheet for each transaction. In accounting, each event generates at least two changes to the financial statements.

In some situations, you might have to make three or more entries to make the balance sheet balance. The next exercise gives you an opportunity to make three entries at once.

EXERCISE 7 ▶
*Gregs rental agency
Part 2*

Continue Working with Greg's Rental Agency

Greg's current balance sheet

Balance sheet			
Assets		**Liabilities**	
Cash	$1,350	Loans	$1,000
Beach hut	$500		
Bicycle	$50	**Equity**	
Ofc. supplies	$100	Paid-in cap.	$1,000
Total assets	**$2,000**	**Total L&E**	**$2,000**

1. Greg's rental agency business really took off. At the end of the year he decided to build an office. The building work cost $100,000. To pay for this Greg took out a $50,000 bank loan and asked friends to invest $50,000 in exchange for equity in his company.

   Help him change the balance sheet to account for the transactions. Remember, Assets = Liabilities + Equity.

Balance sheet			
Assets		**Liabilities**	
_____		_____	
_____			
_____			
_____		Equity	
_____		_____	
Total assets _____		**Total L&E** _____	

continued on next page

EXERCISE 7 ▶
Gregs rental agency
Part 2, continued

Greg's Rental Agency Accounts, part 2, *continued*

2. Greg invests a further $100,000 in the business. He uses the money to buy office furniture for $20,000. He puts the rest into the company's bank account.

Balance sheet

Assets	Liabilities
_____	_____
_____	_____
_____	
_____	
_____	**Equity**
_____	_____
Total	**Total**
assets _____	**L&E** _____

3. Greg decides to sell half the building for $50,000 in cash. With the extra cash he pays back $40,000 of the bank loan.

Make sure the balance sheet balances!

Balance sheet

Assets	Liabilities
_____	_____
_____	_____
_____	
_____	
_____	**Equity**
_____	_____
Total	**Total**
assets _____	**L&E** _____

What financial statements can't tell you

Financial statements measure facts about an entity in units of money. But some facts about an entity and its resources cannot be accurately measured using money.

Facts must be measurable in money

For example, *people* are one of an entity's most important assets. How do you measure how much a company's employees are worth? You can't. Financial statements do not report facts that cannot be reliably measured in money. This fact is called the **money as unit of measurement concept.**

Financial statements are not complete because they don't measure some things. But they do give you valuable information.

EXERCISE 8 ▶
What can be measured?

What Can be Measured?

Which facts are included in a company's financial statements?

❑ 1. The size of a company's bank debt

❑ 2. Employee job satisfaction

❑ 3. The amount of cash a company has in the bank

❑ 4. The company's customer list

❑ 5. The number of cars a company leases

EXERCISE 9 ▶
Cleo's relocation service

Build a Balance Sheet

Record each transaction in the blocks below.

1. Cleo thinks there is a significant opportunity to provide a relocation service to financial analysts. She starts a new company called IBRelocate Inc. and invests $50,000 of her own money in its equity. The new company now has $50,000 in cash.

Assets	Liabilities
	Equity
Total assets _____	Total L&E _____

2. She spends $10,000 of this cash on a car to drive around New York.

Assets	Liabilities
	Equity
Total assets _____	Total L&E _____

continued on next page

EXERCISE 9 ▶

Cleo's relocation service, continued

Build a Balance Sheet, *continued*

3. She then goes to the Bank of New York and takes out a $200,000 loan to really get the business moving. She receives cash from the bank.

Assets	Liabilities
	Equity
Total assets _____	Total L&E _____

4. She purchases a building for $50,000 in the Meat Packing District as her new offices. She pays in cash.

Assets	Liabilities
	Equity
Total assets _____	Total L&E _____

5. Two days after she moves in, the new nightclub Stylo opens next door. The new club stays open until 11am. The music is so loud she cannot use her offices before that time.

Assets	Liabilities
	Equity
Total assets _____	Total L&E _____

Review and Reinforcement

- *The balance sheet must balance.*
  Assets must equal liabilities and equity.

- *Every event has at least two equal entries.*

- *Only facts that can be reliably measured by money appear on the balance sheet.*

Deal #1

your name

value of completed deal

SCORE PAD

1. _____

2. _____

3. _____

4. _____

5. _____

6. _____

7. _____

8. _____

9. _____

10. _____

Total

Close the Deal #1

It's time for you to earn your first "tombstone"! On Wall Street, a tombstone is a clear plastic block announcing a successful deal or project.

You must make $100,000 to earn your tombstone. If you make less than $100,000, review the material before you go on.

1. What is the "unit of measurement" concept?

2. Is a liability a ❏ **source of funding** or a ❏ **resource?**

3. Name two components of equity.

4. If a company's assets are $300,000 and its liabilities are $145,000, what is its equity?

5. How would General Motors account for the threat of a strike at its major manufacturing facility?

6. A company buys a new building for $40,000, two new cars for $30,000 each and new office furniture for $10,000. It also issues $50,000 of equity. Will the company have to borrow additional resources from the bank? Assume the company has no spare cash available. ❏ **Yes**   ❏ **No**

   If yes, how much? _____

7. How often does a balance sheet change?

8. Who has a prior claim on a company's assets?
   ❏ **Equity holders**   ❏ **Liability holders**

9. When you account for a transaction on the balance sheet, at least how many entries do you have to make?

10. What three characteristics must assets have to be included on a company's balance sheet?

3. Divisions within a Balance Sheet

The balance sheet sorts assets and liabilities into current and non-current accounts.

Current assets
Non-current assets

Current liabilities
Non-current liabilities
Equity

Current and non-current accounts

Current Assets

Current assets are short-term assets. They are expected either to turn into cash *within a year* or to be used up *within a year.*

Current:
Lifespan of a year or less

EXAMPLE	
Cash	
Accounts receivable	Money that customers owe but haven't yet paid
Inventory	Goods waiting to be sold

Current Liabilities

Current liabilities are bills or loans that are due within a year. They are generated when a company uses or purchases resources but does not pay for them immediately or borrows money for less than one year.

EXAMPLE	
Accounts payable	Bills for items bought on credit
Loans	Loans due within a year

Non-Current Assets (also Called Long-Term Assets)

Assets which are expected to be useful for longer than a year.

Non-current:
Lifespan of more than a year

EXAMPLE	
Property, plant & equipment (PP&E)	Buildings, land, machinery, furniture
Investments	Long-term ownership stakes or loans to other companies

Non-current:
Lifespan of more
than a year

Non-Current Liabilities (also Called Long-Term Liabilities)

Bills, loans or other obligations that you expect to last longer than **one** year.

EXAMPLE

Long-term debt	A loan due more than a year from now.

EXERCISE 10▶
Long-term vs. short-term

Understanding Long and Short-term Assets and Liabilities

1. Show what each item is by writing in the box:

CA *Current (short-term) asset* **CL** *Current (short-term) liability*
NCA *Non-current (long-term) asset* **NCL** *Non-current (long-term) liability*
  E *Equity*

☐	a. Cash in the cash register
☐	b. A shareholder's investment in a business
☐	c. An electricity bill
☐	d. A three-year bank loan
☐	e. Investment bonds maturing in nine months
☐	f. A factory building
☐	g. Income accumulated from previous years
☐	h. Bills owed to suppliers
☐	i. Money that customers owe you
☐	j. Stocks of goods waiting to be sold
☐	k. Office furniture

2. Describe assets and equity.

3. Which is riskier to own? ☐ **Liabilities** ☐ **Equity**
  Why?

Record assets at purchase cost.

The cost concept

If you record an asset on the balance sheet, you are attaching a dollar value to something that will benefit the company in the future. For example, a company buys an empty plot of land because it expects benefit from the land *in the future.*

However, the market value of an asset may change. The company's plot of land may be worth three times as much next year.

What amount should appear on the balance sheet for the land?

Accounting rules require the land to be recorded at its **original purchase cost** on the company's balance sheet.

EXERCISE 11▶
Sarah's balance sheet

Cost Concept

Sarah, a friend of yours, is an experienced analyst. Over the years she has amassed some valuable assets. To help you practice your accounting skills, she asks you to prepare her balance sheet at the end of the year.

- She has $7,000 in her bank account.

- She owns a Van Gogh sketch which cost her $10,000 and was recently valued at $15,500.

- Her apartment on the Upper West Side was purchased for $150,000. She took out a $110,000 mortgage to help meet the purchase price. The apartment was recently valued at $180,000.

- She owns jewelry worth $14,590. It originally cost $11,000.

1. Write out her balance sheet using the cost concept.

Assets	Liabilities

2. ☐ What is her equity according to the rules of accounting?

3. Does your answer reflect her true net worth?

☐ **Yes** ☐ **No**

4. Why is there a difference between the accounting value of her assets and their market value?

*Financial
analysis tip*

EXERCISE 12▶
Aunt Kate's account

The balance sheet may not be a good indicator of the market value of assets and liabilities. It tells you only what their original purchase price was. The potential sale value of an asset could be higher.

A financial analyst who is trying to determine the sale value of a company's assets and liabilities can't just look at a company's balance sheet. Asset values shown on balance sheets can be misleading.

Understanding Long and Short-term Assets and Liabilities

Your aunt Kate, a successful fashion designer, is having difficulty sorting out her financial situation. She doesn't know accounting, so you offer to help. She says she wants to determine the amount of her total equity, also known as her net worth.

You ask her to list the following:

  all her cash receipts and purchases during the year
  all her assets
  all her liabilities

Here's her list:

- During the year she paid into her bank account her salary of $300,000 (after tax) and her year end bonus of $1,500,000 (after tax). She also purchased a country house for $400,000 in cash and a $10,000 drum kit.
- She owns a $600,000 apartment in midtown New York.
- She has a $400,000 mortgage on the New York apartment.
- She has a $40,000 bank loan payable in six months.
- She owes $3,000 in unpaid household bills.
- She owns $5,000 of Government bonds maturing in six months.
- She owns $50,000 of stocks held as long-term investments.

> **Remember:**
>
> *If she purchased assets with cash, her cash balance will fall.*

As you prepare her balance sheet, round her financial figures to the nearest thousand. Write your answer (to the nearest thousand) in the following table. The template in the margin will help you calculate the ending cash balance. (*Add receipts, add payments, subtract payments from receipts.*)

Cash Balance

Receipts	Payments

Balance Sheet

Assets		Liabilities	
Cash	☐		☐
	☐		☐
Total CA	☐	Total CL	☐
	☐		☐
	☐	Tot. Liab.	☐
	☐	**Equity**	
	☐	Tot. Equity	☐
	☐		
Tot. NCA	☐		
Tot. Assets	☐	Tot. L&E	☐

Deal #2

_____
your name

_____
value of completed deal

SCORE PAD

1. _____

2. _____

3. _____

4. _____

5. _____

6. _____

7. _____

8. _____

9. _____

10. _____

Total

Close the Deal #2

Get another "tombstone" by earning $100,000 or more. If you earn less than $100,000, review the material before you go on.

1. **What is the difference between current and non-current liabilities?**

2. **What are accounts payable? Are they a current or non-current liability?**

3. **What are inventories and are they a current or non-current asset?**

4. At the beginning of the year a company buys a building for $200,000. At the end of the year the accountants are told the building is worth $500,000. What amount do the accountants record on the balance sheet?

5. **If financial analysts are asked to value a company's assets, why can't they just look at the balance sheet?**

6. **Name two current liabilities.**

7. **Name two long-term assets.**

8. **What does the asset side of the balance sheet tell you?**

9. **What does the liabilities and equity side of the balance sheet tell you?**

10. If a company has $40,000 of equity, $50,000 of liabilities and $77,000 of non-cash assets, how much cash is recorded on the balance sheet?

4. Introducing B&J's

You are now going to look at a real-life company's balance sheet. B&J Inc. is a large ice cream manufacturer based in Vermont. On December 31, 1999 its balance sheet looked like this:

B&J's Balance Sheet on 31 December 1999			
	$000s		$000s
Cash & cash equivalents	46,591	Accounts payable	38,915
Accounts receivable	18,833	Current portion LTD and leases	5,627
Inventories of ice cream	13,937	**Total current liabilities**	**44,542**
Other current assets	7,986		
Total current assets	**87,347**	Long-term debt & leases	16,669
		TOTAL LIABILITIES	**61,211**
Property & equipment net	56,557		
Investments	200		
Other non-current assets	6,498		
Total non-current assets	**63,255**	Paid-in capital	40,678
		Retained Earnings	48,713
		TOTAL EQUITY	**89,391**
TOTAL ASSETS	**150,602**	**TOTAL L&E**	**150,602**

Notice how B&J's summarizes some sets of accounts. For example, Property, Plant & Equipment includes all buildings, equipment, and land the company owns.

Preparation for Exercise 14

Examine the B&J's balance sheet. Then update the balance sheet to include the following changes that happened during 2000. Always remember that Assets must equal Liabilities + Equity. There are lots of flows in and out of the cash account so use the table on the side to keep account of them.

EXERCISE 13▶
B&J's balance sheet

A Real-Life Balance Sheet

Note: all figures in thousands ($000)

- B&J's received $2,000 in cash from people who owed it money (accounts receivable). Hint: cash increases, accounts receivable decreases.

- The Company bought 50,000 gallons of milk to turn into ice cream inventory. The farmer who sold them the milk gave them credit for the entire price of $5,000. The Company then logged this $5,000 in accounts payable. Hint: inventory increases and accounts payable also increases.

- The Company purchased a new property for $10,000 paying for it in cash. Hint: cash falls and property and equipment rises.

- The Company issued $10,000 of new shares and received cash. Hint: paid-in capital rises and cash rises.

- The Company used $5,000 of the cash it raised from its share issue to pay down its long-term debt. Hint: cash falls and long-term debt falls.

- The company sold $200 of its investments for cash. Hint: cash rises and investments fall.

- Assume all other accounts remain the same.

Fill out B&J's balance sheet.

B&J's balance sheet on 31 December 2000

ASSETS	$000s	LIABILITIES	$000s
Cash & cash equivalents		Accounts payable	
Accounts receivable		Other	
Inventories of ice cream		**Total current liabilities**	
Other current assets			
Total current assets		Long-term debt	
		Other L-T liabilities	
Property & equipment net		**Total non-current liabs.**	
Investments		**TOTAL LIABILITIES**	
Other non-current assets			
Total non-current assets		Paid-in capital	
		Retained Earnings	
		TOTAL EQUITY	
TOTAL ASSETS		**TOTAL L&E**	

Cash Balance

Receipts	Payments

New meanings for old world

This is tricky...

...but it helps organize your work

Journal Entries: An Easy Way of Ensuring A = L + E

The next part of this course is **crucial for your understanding of accounting.** Start by **setting aside your current definitions of "Debit" and "Credit."**

Consumers think of credit as a good thing. **For a business** owner, a credit on the books represents **an increase in a liability** or equity or a reduction in an asset.

You'll have to work with **these terms until you are** comfortable making journal entries and you **understand why debits** must equal credits.

> ### New meanings for two old words: Debit and Credit
>
> | Assets | Liabilities & Equity |
> |---|---|
> | Increases = Debits | Increases = Credits |
> | Decreases = Credits | Decreases = Debits |

Journal entries help you **organize changes you make to the balance** sheet.

Assets	=	Liabilities	+	Equity
+ Debit ǀ – Credit		– Debit ǀ + Credit		– Debit ǀ + Credit

Total debits always must **equal total credits.**

EXAMPLE

Examples of journal entries using debits (**Dr**) and credits (**Cr**):

B&J receives $2,000 in **cash from people who owned it** money.

Debit	Cash	$2,000	
Credit	Accounts receivable		$2,000

B&J issues **$10,000 worth of new shares and receives cash.**

Debit	Cash	$10,000	
Credit	Paid-in capital		$10,000

B&J uses **$5,000 of its cash to pay down its long-term debt.**

Debit	Long-term debt	$5,000	
Credit	Cash		$5,000

Note: **Debit** is often written as **Dr**, **Credit** as **Cr**

EXERCISE 14 ▶
Journal entries

Journal Entries

You are going to record several debit and credit transactions for B&J. Write out the proper debits and credits. Include the name of the account. The templates at the bottom of the page will help you.

Debits are traditionally written on the left and credits on the right.

Example
The company purchases $2,000 of inventory using cash.

Debit	Inventory	$2,000	
Credit	Cash		$2,000

1. The company issues $1,000 worth of shares for cash.

   Debit _____

   Credit _____

2. The company buys $4,000 of chocolate (inventory) for cash.

   Debit _____

   Credit _____

3. The company purchases new equipment worth $10,000. It takes out an $8,000 loan (lasting five years) to do this. It pays for the remaining $2,000 with cash.

   Debit _____

   Credit _____

   Credit _____

4. The company buys a van for $5,000. It uses $3,000 of cash and takes out a short-term loan to pay the remaining $2,000.

   Debit _____

   Credit _____

   Credit _____

For more debit and credit practice, turn to Appendix A in the back of the book.

Use these T-accounts to help find answers

Assets		=	Liabilities		+	Equity	
+ Debit	– Credit		– Debit	+ Credit		– Debit	+ Credit

Use this form to help track journal entries

Account	Debits	Credits
Dr _____	_____	
Cr _____		_____
Dr _____	_____	
Cr _____		_____
Dr _____	_____	
Cr _____		_____
Dr _____	_____	
Cr _____		_____
Dr _____	_____	
Cr _____		_____
Dr _____	_____	
Cr _____		_____
Dr _____	_____	
Cr _____		_____
Dr _____	_____	
Cr _____		_____

Check your work.
Do debits = credits?

Total debits _____

Total credits _____

Close the Deal #3

Get another "tombstone" by earning $50,000 or more. If you score less than $50,000, review the material before you go on.

1. Put yourself in B&J's shoes when they first set up their company. Assume they made the following transactions in the first month the company was set up:

   a. B&J's owners each put in $40,000 cash to get the company started. In return for their investments they each received shares.

   b. They also went to their local bank to take out a loan for $50,000. They received cash.

   c. They purchased two ice cream-making machines for $10,000 each in cash.

   d. They also purchased $4,000 of ingredients including 500 gallons of milk from the local dairy (record as inventory). They asked the farmer to give them credit for this order (record as an account payable).

   e. During the first week they bought a truck. They paid $2,000 in cash.

   f. They purchased an old garage to house their ice-cream making operations. The garage cost $10,000 in cash.

   g. During the second week they ordered more milk from the dairy for $500. The dairy said they must wait for the delivery of the milk. They did not have to pay for the milk until it was delivered.

   h. In the third week they bought a computer for their accounting. The computer cost $1,000 in cash.

   i. In the fourth week one of the ice cream-making machines broke down.

   j. In the fifth week they repaid $20,000 of the $50,000 loan to the bank.

Record these transactions on the left. Then build their balance sheet at the end of the month.

B&J's Balance Sheet

Assets	Liabilities & Equity

continued on next page

Deal #3

_____
your name

_____
value of completed deal

SCORE PAD

1. _____

2. _____

3. _____

4. _____

5. _____

Total

Debits and credits got you down?

Do the extra exercises in Appendix A!

Close the Deal #3, *continued*

1. **Name four sources of funds.**

   a. [   ]   b. [   ]

   c. [   ]   d. [   ]

3. **If a company increases its total resources what must it also do?**

   [   ]

4. **What is the difference between a current and a non-current asset?**

   [   ]

5. **Name two of B&J's current assets.**

   a. [   ]   b. [   ]

Debit – Credit Workout

If you need more practice with debits and credits, do the exercises in Appendix A.

The Income Statement
1. Overview

The income statement is a summary…

…of revenue

…and expenses

…ending with net income

The income statement shows you how a company has performed over a period of time. All companies prepare income statements annually, at the same time that they prepare their balance sheets. Companies traded on the US stock market also provide quarterly statements.

Unlike the balance sheet which records conditions at one instant in time (usually the end of the fiscal year), the income statement is a **summary**. It summarizes information about revenues and expenses that have accumulated over an entire time period, usually a whole fiscal year.

The income statement records the sales a company generated during the accounting period and the costs it incurred to generate those sales. It has several sections.

The income statement

Sales made in the **whole accounting period**	**Sales**
Production expenses generated by the sales	**Cost of Goods Sold**
Overhead expenses during the **whole period**	**Sales, General and Administrative Costs**
Infrequent or unusual income for the **whole period**	**Other Income**
Infrequent or unusual expenses for the **whole period**	**Other Expenses**
Income from cash and investments or the cost of debt for the **whole period**	**Interest Expense or Income**
Tax a company estimates it will have to pay on the period's profit	**Tax**
Net income (income after all expenses) generated over the **whole period**	**Net Income**

EXERCISE 15▶
Chugger's

Build an Income Statement

Chris, the owner of a new cafe bar called Chugger's, sits down to do his accounts. In front of him are scraps of paper in no particular order. He needs to sort them into a proper income statement which will show how much business he has done over the last month:

■ He estimated his tax bill for the month would be $4,000.

■ He received a $2,000 bill from his bank for last month's interest.

■ His first month's sales, general and admin costs were $3,000.

■ His cost of goods sold was $10,000 for the month.

■ He made $50,000 in sales during the month, all in cash.

■ He had no other income or expenses.

Help him by building his income statement using the above information. Some subtotals are already included.

Income statement for Chugger's

Sales	
Direct costs of sales	
Gross profit	40,000

Hint: gross profit = sales minus direct costs

Sales, general and administrative costs	
Operating profit	37,000

Hint: operating profit = gross profit minus SG&A costs

Other income or expense	

Hint: if any. Remember the entity concept.

Interest income and expense	
Profit before tax	35,000
Tax	
Net Income	

Hint: all revenue and income less all expenses

2. Revenue

The income statement

Do sales = cash?

Not necessarily!

Manufacture, deliver, *then* record the sale

The first section of the income statement deals with *revenues.*

Sales Made Do Not Always Equal Cash Received

The problem in using the receipt of cash to record sales (cash accounting) is that it does not capture sales made on credit. Imagine a store like Macy's measuring its sales by the amount of cash it collects. Because many customers use credit cards, cash accounting would not give Macy's management an accurate picture of how many sales they made on one day.

Sales Are Recorded When They Are Delivered

An important aspect of GAAP accounting is the question: *when should a company recognize revenue from a sale?* Under GAAP, sales are recognized **when the goods are delivered** to the customer. Not when they are manufactured, not when the contract is signed, not when the cash is received.

If you sell a service, record the revenue **when the service is performed.**

Goods manufactured	Goods stored in warehouse	Goods delivered	Cash received

Time → Accounting recognizes sales here

EXAMPLE

A grocer delivers $30 worth of bananas to a local store on credit. His cash does not increase but he successfully generates $30 of revenues. He is certain the store will pay and wants to record the benefit of these sales in his accounts.

	Monday	**Tuesday**	**Wednesday**
	Grocer agrees to sell $30 of bananas.	Grocer delivers $30 of bananas.	Grocer gets paid $30 in cash for bananas.
Sales	$0	+ $30	$0
Cash	$0	$0	+ $30

By recording the sales on delivery rather then waiting until he receives the cash, his financial statements better reflect the true performance of his business.

EXERCISE 16 ▶
New York supermarket

Recognizing Sales

1. A New York supermarket telephoned B&J and ordered 2,000 tubs of pralines and cream @ $1.50 per tub, to be delivered in a month. How would B&J account for the transaction on their income statement that day? Assume each tub cost $1 to make.

2. When B&J's delivered the ice cream to the supermarket, they were paid $3,000 in cash. How would B&J account for this transaction on their income statement?

3. If the supermarket paid for the ice cream before B&J had delivered it, would B&J record the sales on their income statement?
   ❑ Yes   ❑ No

3. Expenses

The income statement

The income statement separates normal business expenses into two categories:

❑ Direct production costs (also called the cost of goods sold or **COGS**)

❑ Sales, general and administrative costs, or **SG&A**

> Record expenses…

> …when you recognize the revenue

> What about stuff like insurance?

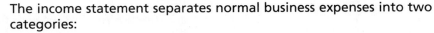

MATCHING EXPENSES TO REVENUES

When you record revenues, you also record (or *match*) the expenses that directly helped to generate that revenue.

Some costs don't relate directly to revenue

Cash spent on manufacture	Sale recorded Costs of manufacture expensed (recorded) in COGS
Goods manufactured	**Goods delivered**

Time

Some costs don't relate directly to revenue

Some costs cannot be directly matched to revenue. For example, insurance expense on a factory building occurs regardless of how many orders the sales team generates. In these circumstances, companies expense (record on their books) the insurance during the period it was used.

Expenses don't always equal cash costs

A business can incur costs by purchasing goods and services on credit. So expenses can be recorded without using up cash.

A company can also buy goods and services and store them for future use (think of an insurance policy, for example, or inventory). They have spent cash, but they don't record an expense on their income statement.

EXERCISE 17▶
Disneyland

Matching Expenses with Revenue

B&J buys $100,000 of milk in March. In April it uses the milk to manufacture 100 tons of ice cream. It sells all 100 tons to Disneyland for $200,000. Disney takes delivery of half the ice cream in May, a quarter in June and a quarter in July. B&J receives cash from Disneyland in August.

1. Track the cash receipts, payments and revenue on the following table:

	Mar	Apr	May	Jun	Jul	Aug
Revenue						
Milk expenses						
Change in cash						

2. B&J buys a 5-month insurance policy in March for $600. The policy starts in May. Track the insurance expense recognition and the change in cash each month.

	Mar	Apr	May	Jun	Jul	Aug	Sep
Insurance expense							
Change in cash							

The Conservatism Concept

Accounting is conservative when recording revenue and losses.

Accounting recognizes revenue when it is **reasonably certain.** Accounting recognizes losses when they are **reasonably possible** *(GAAP calls it "reasonably determinable.")*

Don't overlook this concept!

EXERCISE 18▶
Kalvin Kleen

Conservatism and Recognition

Kalvin Kleen recently opened a sock warehouse in New York. Business was brisk in the first few months after opening. One day he received a call from a large uptown department store who wanted to order $2,000 worth of men's socks. Kalvin had heard that the store's buyer is notoriously fickle and changes his mind like the weather.

1. In order to fulfill the concepts of realization and conservatism, when does Kalvin recognize the $2,000 of revenue?

❏ When the socks are ordered   ❏ When the socks are delivered
❏ When Kalvin receives the cash

continued on next page

Conservatism and Recognition continued

In the end the department store did want the socks. Kalvin dispatched them by courier. At five o'clock that day the department store still had not received the order. Eventually the courier company called and said that their messenger had disappeared without a trace that afternoon. The messenger was known to have a penchant for Kalvin Kleen socks.

2. Kalvin would like to wait until next month before he accounts for the loss. After all, the missing socks may turn up. Under the rules of accounting, when should Kalvin account for the loss of the socks?

   ❑ The same day   ❑ Next week   ❑ Next month

   Hint: remember the conservatism concept and be conservative

3. Above Kalvin's shop is an apartment. Kalvin decided to rent the apartment as a source of additional revenue. A new tenant moved in on June 1 and paid Kalvin $6,000 for six months rent upfront in cash. When should Kalvin account for this revenue?

   How much in:

   June?   _____   July?   _____

   August?   _____   September? _____

   October?   _____   November? _____

COGS tends to fall and rise with the level of sales

Costs of goods sold (COGS) represent costs that are directly related to the manufacture of a product or service. These costs/expenses tend to rise or fall according to how much is sold during the accounting period.

COGS is linked to sales…

Examples   The cost of milk that B&J uses to make ice cream.

The cost of the labor that mixes the ice cream.

SG&A costs tend to remain stable

Sales, general and administrative costs are costs or expenses that a company incurs to keep the organization running. SG&A costs are not directly related to production.

…SG&A isn't

Examples   Maintenance costs for the president's company-owned BMW.

The salaries of employees in the accounting department.

EXERCISE 19 ▶
The clueless bookkeeper

COGS or SG&A?

At the end of the year, B&J's owners ask you to prepare an income statement to reflect the business the company did during the year. Your bookkeeper asks you the following questions.

1. "I have a bill here for milk. In which cost category should I put it?"

   ❏ COGS   ❏ SG&A

2. "The bill for my salary has come in. Where should it go?"

   ❏ COGS   ❏ SG&A

3. "Should I put interest expense into COGS or SG&A?"

   ❏ COGS   ❏ SG&A

4. "Here's the printer's bill for the sales brochure. Where does it go?"

   ❏ COGS   ❏ SG&A

5. "We bought a $100,000 ice cream-making machine using cash last year. What journal entries should I make?"

   Debit _____ _____

   Credit _____   _____

Unusual or infrequent income and expenses

Other income and expenses

This category includes the other income and expenses not included in the COGS or SG&A category. Other income and expenses are unusual or infrequent items that are not part of a company's normal operations.

Example   Gain on the sale of equipment

Interest income and expense

Interest income   Cash in the bank can generate interest income. The more cash a company has, the higher its interest income. Interest income can also be generated from investments.

Interest expense   Outstanding loans generate interest expense. The larger the loan, the greater the interest expense.

Net income increases equity, not cash

At the end of an accounting period, the accountant adds net income to retained earnings on the balance sheet. The increase in retained earnings increases a company's equity balance. As revenues increase net income, they help to increase retained earnings (equity) in the business. As expenses decrease net income, they decrease equity.

Net income is not cash income. A company can recognize revenue before it receives any cash, and it can record expenses before it pays any cash.

4. Journal Entries on the I/S

More debits and credits…

An easy way to organize your additions and subtractions to the income statement is to use journal entries.

■ Expenses or costs are **debits** on the income statement

■ Revenue or sales and income are **credits** on the income statement

Income Statement		Equity	
Increases	= credits	Increases	= credits
Decreases	= debits	Decreases	= debits

Notice that the income statement and the equity accounts use debits and credits the same way, *because net income and retained earnings are linked.*

…this time on the Income Statement

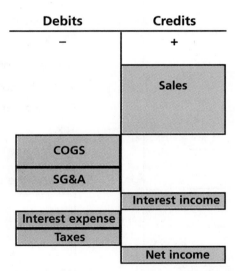

EXERCISE 20▶
Credits and debits

Increase (+) or decrease (–) in equity? Debit or Credit?

Try this exercise to get more insights into credits and debits on the income statement.

	+ or – in equity?	Debit or credit?
1. An increase in sales is		
2. An increase in costs is		
3. Tax expense is		
4. Interest income is		

Need more credit and dedit help? Go to Appendix A.

Deal #4

_____
your name

_____
value of completed deal

SCORE PAD

1. _____

2. _____

3. _____

4. _____

5. _____

6. _____

7. _____

8. _____

9. _____

10. _____

Total

Close the Deal #4

Win another "tombstone" by earning $100,000 or more. If you earn less than $100,000, review the material before you go on.

1. When does a company account for revenue?

2. Does the income statement measure changes in cash or equity?
   ❏ **Cash**   ❏ **Equity**

3. As a company's cash balance grows, what will probably happen to its interest income?   ❏ **Rise**   ❏ **Fall**   ❏ **Remain unchanged**

4. You set up a curtain-making business. In one year you made 100 curtains for $10 each. You sold them all for $50 each. Your accountant's charges were $1,000 and you paid yourself as chief executive $2,000. Your interest income on the cash in your bank account was $500. You also purchased a 2-year insurance policy for $200. You pay tax on your profits at 50%. Prepare your income statement for that year:

Curtain business income statement

Revenue	_____
COGS	_____
Gross profit	_____
SG&A	_____
Operating profit	_____
Interest income	_____
Earnings before tax	_____
Tax	_____
Net income	_____

5. What is the conservatism concept in accounting?

6. What does COGS stand for? _____

7. What does SG&A stand for?   _____

8. If you reduce your bank loans, what will probably happen to your interest income?   ❏ **Rise**   ❏ **Fall**   ❏ **Remain unchanged**

9. If you buy inventory on credit what happens to your cash balance?   ❏ **Rise**   ❏ **Fall**   ❏ **Remain unchanged**

10. Which accounts would change in Question 9?

Links

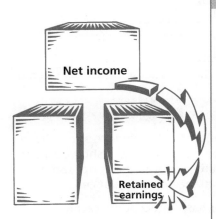

Financial analysts must understand the *links* between the balance sheet and income statement. Many activities change both the income statement and the balance sheet at the same time. You'll now look at some of the important links between these financial statements.

NET INCOME AND RETAINED EARNINGS

The most important relationship between the income statement and balance sheet is the link between net income and retained earnings .

During the year a company creates net income by generating more revenue and income than expenses. The company then adds its net income for the year to retained earnings. If net income is negative, the loss is subtracted from retained earnings.

Net income, dividends and retained earnings

Dividends are paid out of *retained earnings,* not net income. A good way of understanding the flows in and out of retained earnings is to use **B-A-S-E** analysis.

B-A-S-E analysis is a simple technique to help you understand the flows into and out of an account over a period of time.

B	balance at **B**eginning of period	150
A	**A**dditions during the period	+ 60
S	**S**ubtractions during the period	– 10
E	The balance at the **E**nd of the period	200

B A S E
analysis:
a useful tool

> **EXAMPLE**
>
> As of December 31, 1998, B&J's had retained $45,328,000 earnings in its business from previous years. In the year ending December 31, 1999, B&J generated $3,385,000 net income. It paid no dividends during the year.
>
> #### B&J's retained earnings (B A S E analysis)
>
> | | | |
> |---|---|---|
> | B | Beginning balance | $45,328,000 |
> | A | Additions | $3,385,000 |
> | S | Subtractions | $0 |
> | E | Ending balance | $48,713,000 |

You can use this information to establish the flows in and out of B&J's retained earnings account in 2000.

BASE Analysis

Assume that in the year January 1 to December 31 2000 B&J's generated $10,567,000 of net income. it also decided to pay $6,000,500 in dividends to its shareholders. Now fill in the following B-A-S-E analysis table:

B	Beginning balance, retained earnings	48,713,000
	Beginning balance from the previous year's info, above	
A	Additions	
S	Subtractions	
E	Ending balance	

REVENUE AND CURRENT ASSETS

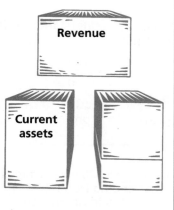

Another important link connects revenue and the balance sheet. When a company records a sale, its net income goes up. Link 1 showed you that if net income goes up, so does equity. If equity goes up, something else has to change to make the balance sheet balance.

The account that changes will be either cash or accounts receivable (A/R).

- **When customers pay on the spot, cash goes up.**
- **When the company gives credit, A/R goes up.**

Either way, the increase in equity is balanced.

Think of the link another way. If a company makes a sale, what happens?

Cash or A/R rises . . .
 Therefore total assets rise . . .
  Therefore you need a balancing entry.

Assets | L & E

But wait! The sale added revenue to the income statement, which...

Increases net income, which . . .
 Increases retained earnings, which . . .
  Increases equity.

Assets | L & E

Now the balance sheet balances again.

More about accounts receivable

When you deliver goods to a customer, you recognize the revenue by recording it on the income statement. But what if the customer buys on credit and pays later?

If you record the sales on your income statement . . .

...your equity will rise . . .

...therefore you need a balancing entry . . .

...so record the credit sales as accounts receivable on the asset side of the balance sheet.

EXERCISE 22▶
Ice cream sales

Revenue and the Balance Sheet

1. B&J sold $50,000 of ice cream during the year. $30,000 of the sale was on credit. The rest was paid for in cash.

   Debit _____ _____

   Debit _____ _____

   Credit _____ _____

   Hint: increase cash and accounts receivable

2. During the year customers with outstanding accounts paid $25,000 to B&J. Hint: increase cash and reduce A/R.

   Debit _____ _____

   Credit _____ _____

3. [   ] Assuming no other sales, what would be the balance (the remaining amount) of accounts receivable after question 2?

4. What happened to equity when the $25,000 was paid in question 2?

   ❑ Nothing; equity already went up when the sale was recorded

   ❑ Equity went up by $25,000

   ❑ Equity went down to balance the drop in accounts receivable

COGS AND INVENTORIES

When a company records cost of goods sold on its income statement, net income falls. If net income falls, retained earnings fall and equity also goes down. If equity falls, something else has to change so that the balance sheet will balance. The account that changes is inventory.

■ *When COGS goes up, inventory goes down.*

Think of the link another way. If goods are delivered from inventory to a customer, what happens?

Inventory falls . . .

    . . . Therefore total assets fall . . .

      . . . Therefore you need a balancing entry.

But wait! The cost of inventory hits COGS in the income statement only when the goods are delivered and the sales are recognized.

Therefore, when inventory falls . . .

    . . . COGS goes up, which . . .

      . . . Decreases retained earnings, which . . .

      . . . Decreases equity.

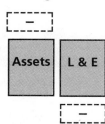

Now the balance sheet balances again. The journal entries look like this:

Debit: Increase cost of goods sold
Credit: Decrease inventory

EXERCISE 23▶
Avocado Explosion

COGS and Inventories

B&J decided to launch a new ice cream called Avocado Explosion. They bought the following ingredients:

- 2,000 worth of avocados, paid for with an IOU. *Hint: increase A/P and inventories.*

- 5,000 worth of milk, paid for with an IOU to the farmer
  Hint: increase accounts payable

Then they delivered $3,000 worth of Avocado Explosion to a trendy restaurant in New York. *Hint: increase COGS, decrease inventory.*

B&J charged $5,000 for the ice cream. The restaurant paid $2,500 in cash and said they would pay the balance in one month.

1. After the transaction, what would the balance sheet and income statement look like? (Assume no taxes are paid.)

Assets	L & E	Income Statement
Cash	Acct Pay	Sales
Inv.		COGS
Acct. Recv.	Ret earnings	
Total	**Total**	**Net Income**

2. [   ] What is B&J's gross profit on the sale?

Interest income and expense

Cash and investments

Debt

INTEREST AND THE BALANCE SHEET

Interest expense

Long term liabilities are mostly debt accounts. A company is charged interest on its outstanding loans, which are recorded on the balance sheet. The larger a company's outstanding loans, the larger its interest expense, assuming interest rates stay constant.

Interest income

The amount of a company's interest income depends on the amount of its interest-bearing assets. These include:

- Cash in deposit accounts
- Loans to other entities
- Bonds

The larger a company's interest-bearing accounts, the larger its interest income, assuming interest rates stay constant. Interest income is shown on the income statement after the company's operating profit line, usually above the interest expense account.

EXERCISE 24▶
Interest

Interest Income and Expense

1. If a company increases the loans on its balance sheet, what will happen to the interest expense on its income statement?

   ❏ Increase ❏ Decrease ❏ Stay the same

2. Suppose a company's interest income rises and interest rates stay the same. What does this suggest about its interest-bearing assets like bonds and cash in deposit accounts?

   ❏ They increased ❏ Decreased ❏ Stayed the same

3. A company took out a $40,000 loan at the beginning of the year. The bank charges interest at 7% per annum. What would be the journal entries for interest expense at the end of the year assuming the company paid the bank in cash?

   Debit _____ _____

   Credit _____   _____

4. Another company had an exceptionally good year. At year end it put $67,000 on deposit at its bank at 6.2% interest. How would journal entries record the interest at the end of next year?

   Debit _____ _____

   Credit _____   _____

EXERCISE 25 ▶
The links

Links Between Balance Sheet and Income Statement

1. Using the B&J's balance sheet below, create an income statement and new balance sheet for 2000. *All numbers in thousands.*

- B&J bought milk for $150,000. The farmer gave them credit.
  Hint: Increase inventories and increase accounts payable.

- B&J bought a new machine for $80,000 cash.

- During the year they paid their management $49,000 in cash.
  Hint: Increase SG&A

- The bank charged 12% on their existing loans. They paid in cash.

- During the year, B&J generated $200,890 in revenue. $10,000 was on credit, the rest was in cash.

- B&J's sales cost them $130,000.
  Hint: Reduce inventory and increase COGS

- B&J's other administration costs were $10,890, paid in cash.
  Hint: Increase SG&A.

- B&J's paid dividends of $1,000 in cash. Hint: debit Ret. earnings.

- Assume they recorded and paid $3,851 of tax in cash during 1996.

- **Assume all other accounts remain the same.**

Use journal entries, the cash balance template and B A S E analysis to calculate inventories and retained earnings.

Continue on Page 46 after you finish Question 1

Use this form to help track journal entries

	Account	Debits	Credits
Dr	_____	_____	
Cr	_____		_____
Dr	_____	_____	
Cr	_____		_____
Dr	_____	_____	
Cr	_____		_____
Dr	_____	_____	
Cr	_____		_____
Dr	_____	_____	
Cr	_____		_____
Dr	_____	_____	
Cr	_____		_____
Dr	_____	_____	
Cr	_____		_____
Dr	_____	_____	
Cr	_____		_____

Check your work.
Do debits = credits?

Total debits _____

Total credits _____

B&J's Balance Sheet
on 31 December 1999

	$000s		$000s
Cash & cash equivalents	46,591	Accounts payable	38,915
Accounts receivable	18,833	Current portion LTD and leases	5,627
Inventories of ice cream	13,937	**Total current liabilities**	**44,542**
Other current assets	7,986		
Total current assets	**87,347**	Long-term debt & leases	16,669
		TOTAL LIABILITIES	**61,211**
Property & equipment net	56,557		
Investments	200		
Other non-current assets	6,498		
Total non-current assets	**63,255**	Paid-in capital	40,678
		Retained Earnings	48,713
		TOTAL EQUITY	**89,391**
TOTAL ASSETS	**150,602**	**TOTAL L&E**	**150,602**

Retained earnings

Beg

Add

Sub

End

Inventories

Beg

Add

Sub

End

Cash Balance

Receipts	**Payments**

B&J's Income Statement on 31 December 2000

Revenue/sales

Cost of goods sold

Gross profit

SG&A

Operating profit

Interest expense

Profit before tax

Task

Net income

B&J's Balance Sheet on 31 December 2000

ASSETS	$000s	LIABILITIES	$000s
Total curr. assets		**Total curr. liabs**	
Total NCA		**Total NCL**	
		TOT. LIABILITIES	
Total NCA		**TOTAL EQUITY**	
TOTAL ASSETS		**TOTAL L&E**	

Links Between B/S and I/S, *continued*

2a. Where are dividends paid from?

❑ Retained earnings   ❑ Net income   ❑ Sales

A company pays cash dividends of $28,000. What journal entries does it make?

Dr _____   _____

Cr _____   _____

b. A company has accumulated $3,200,894 of earnings from previous years. It generates $134,892 of income during the year, and pays $90,891 in dividends during the year. What are its year-end retained earnings?

Year-end retained earnings _____

3a. Name two links between the balance sheet and the income statement.

Link 1.

Link 2.

b. What's the difference between accounts receivable and accounts payable ?

4a. A company buys $100,000 of inventory on credit. What journal entries does it make?

Dr _____   _____

Cr _____   _____

b. A company delivers goods that cost $3,589 to produce. What journal entries must it make?

Dr _____   _____

Cr _____   _____

End of Part 1

You have reached the end of Part 1. Now take the *Checkout Test* and score at least 90%. If you do not score at least 90%, you should review Part 1 again and then retake the test.

Don't go on to Part 2 until you have taken the test and scored at least 90%. If you don't know this material, you probably won't be able to complete the assignment at the end of the book.

Turn the page to start the test.

Checkout Test for Part 1

This test will probe your understanding of basic accounting. You should meet standards (90% or $900,000) in this test before moving to Part 2.

Section 1

You are the Chief Financial Officer for PepsiCo. Your bookkeeper gives you the information below to build year-end financial statements for 2000.

Figures are in millions.

❏ Create PepsiCo's income statement for the year ending Dec. 31, 2000.

❏ Create a balance sheet for PepsiCo as of Dec. 31, 2000.

**Fill in the blank forms on the opposite page.
Round your answers to the nearest million**

Make your first million

_____
your name

_____
value of completed deal

Income statement

1. Sales for the year were $20,438.
2. Other operating costs were equal to 0.675% of sales for the year.
3. COGS was $7,943.
4. Interest income was $76, interest expense $221.
5. PepsiCo recorded $1,027 worth of income taxes during the year.
6. SG&A costs were equal to 44.7% of sales for the year.
7. Equity income was $130.

Balance sheet *(as of December 31, 2000, except when otherwise noted)*

1. Just before PepsiCo paid its dividend, the company's cash and cash equivalents on its balance sheet amounted to $2,126.
   Hint: Remember to remove dividends from the cash balance.
2. Other current liabilities amounted to $120.
3. PepsiCo owed $2,346 in long-term debt. Other long-term liabilities were $4,908.
4. Customers owed PepsiCo $1,799.
5. PepsiCo paid a dividend of $796
   Hint: Use this to help calculate ending retained earnings and cash.
6. Retained earnings were $4,878 at the beginning of the year.
7. PepsiCo had short-term bills (*accounts payable*) outstanding of $3,815.
8. On December 31, PepsiCo had $905 worth of inventories.
9. Other current assets were $570.
10. Property plant and equipment was $5,438.
12. PepsiCo owned $2,978 of long-term investments.
13. Other long-term assets amounted to $5,319.
14. Paid-in capital was $984.

Checkout test continued on next page

PepsiCo's Income Statement (in millions)
Year ending December 31, 2000

Net Sales _____

Cost of Sales _____

Gross Profit _____

Selling General and Administrative Expenses _____

Other Operating Costs _____

Operating Profit _____

Equity Income _____

Interest Income _____

Interest Expense _____

Earnings Before Tax _____

Provision for Income Taxes _____

Net Income _____

PepsiCo's Balance Sheet (in millions)
Year ending December 31, 2000

ASSETS		LIABILITIES AND SHAREHOLDERS' EQUITY	
Cash and cash equivalents	_____	Accounts payable	_____
Accounts receivable	_____	Other current liabilities	_____
Inventories	_____	**Total current liabilities**	_____
Other current assets	_____		
Total current assets	_____	Long-term debt	_____
Investments	_____	Other long-term liabilities	_____
PP&E	_____	**Total liabilities**	_____
Other long-term assets	_____	Paid-in capital	_____
		Retained earnings	_____
		Total shareholders' equity	_____
Total assets	_____	**Total liabilities and shareholders' equity**	_____

Section 2

1. Explain the meaning of the matching concept:

2. In 1999 B&J made $400,000 in sales, 35% on credit and 65% for cash. Fill in the journal entries:

   Dr   _____   _____

   Dr   _____   _____

   Cr   _____   _____

3. What does **GAAP** stand for?

4. Which personal assets of Deutsche Lazard's employees are included in the financial statements of Deutsche Lazard?

5. Explain "Accounting represents information about an entity."

6. Name four current assets or current liabilities:

   a. _____

   b. _____

   c. _____

   d. _____

7. Describe what equity represents on the balance sheet.

8. Name two things financial statements cannot tell you:

   a. _____

   b. _____

Checkout test continued on next page

Score Pad

Section 1

Income statement correct
Worth $300,000

Balance sheet correct
Worth $300,000

Your score: ▢

Section 2

Each correct question is worth $25,000. All parts of the question must be correct.

Your score: ▢

Section 3

Each correct question is worth $25,000. All parts of the question must be correct.

Your score: ▢

TOTAL SCORE ▢

Section 3

1. What is the difference between cost of goods sold and sales, general and administrative costs?

2. The balance sheet reflects operating activities over the year.
   ❏ True   ❏ False

3. Which balance sheet account is net income added to?

4. What does the income statement measure?
   ❏ Changes in equity   ❏ Changes in cash

5. When are revenues recognized?

6. Describe non-cash current assets.

7. How is inventory linked to the income statement?

8. If a company's cash balance grows, what will happen to:

   Interest income _____

   Interest expense _____

End of Checkout Test for Part 1

If you don't earn $900,000 on this test, go back and review the concepts you missed.

Part Two:

Accounting for Financial Analysis

About Part 2

Detective work on Coca-Cola . . .

Now you'll start to apply your basic accounting skills by analyzing the Coca-Cola Company's financial statements. Like a detective, you'll find crucial information, which you'll use to understand more about the company's performance.

What You'll Learn

When you finish Part 2, you will understand what a company's financial statements can tell you. You will know:

- **What you can find in a company's financial statements;**
- **What the individual accounts on the balance sheet and income statement tell you;**
- **How to calculate a cash flow statement;**
- **What the numbers tell you about the company's business.**

. . . develops your financial accounting skills

Introduction to Coca-Cola's Annual Report

You'll find Coca-Cola's financial statements on page 195. You'll be referencing the information frequently for the rest of this book. Here is a summary of its key elements:

P 44 – 45	Selected financial data
P. 46 – 47	The balance sheet
P. 48	The income statement
P. 49	The cash flow statement
P. 51 – 66	Notes to the accounts

Look for This Icon

Every time you see this icon, you'll be looking for information in Coca-Cola's annual report.

Take a look...

Here We Go!

Turn the page and let's get started.

*Financial
analysis tip*

Your Information Source

One of your major sources of information about a company are the financial statements and other information in its *annual report.* In Part 2, you will extract and interpret key data from Coca-Cola's annual report, skills every analyst must know how to use.

Different annual reports will have different layouts. However, most companies with publicly traded shares will include the information listed below.

Guide to the Typical Annual Report

Section	Description
Financial highlights, Table of contents	Opening remarks
Chairman's letter to shareholders	Overview of the company's activities during the year
	General statements about the company's future plans and strategy
Review of operations	A rich source of information for you. May include a breakdown of revenues and profitability by region and sector, a clear idea of investment plans and a lot of information about individual divisions.
Financials	The most important part for you. Financials are divided into into three sections:
1. Financial commentary	Includes useful information about ratios, margins and subsidiaries.
2. Financial statements	A summary of the company's financial statements for the full year. They include:
	Income statement *Balance sheet* *Cash flow statement*
3. Notes to the financial statements	Important: they include additional data about accounts and describe the company's significant accounting policies.
Report of independent auditors	The auditors check to see if the accounts are a fair and true reflection of the company's activities during that year.
Board of directors	Key management and the board of directors

The Balance Sheet
1. Current Assets

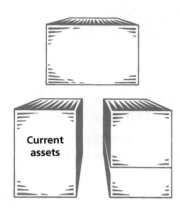

Current assets

CASH AND CASH EQUIVALENTS

Nearly all companies need cash to run their business.

- **They need cash to pay salaries and bills.**
- **A retail store needs to give change when making sales.**

Most companies' cash balances are small compared to their annual sales. They keep just enough ready cash to run their operations smoothly.

However, the cash situation changes when a company wants to make a big investment. Say Coca-Cola wanted to acquire a large bottling plant for $500 million. Coca-Cola may amass a large amount of cash in preparation for the acquisition. Then the amount of cash on the balance sheet would be far greater than needed just for everyday operations.

When a company is not using its cash balance it may invest its cash in very low risk *liquid* (*easily sold*) securities so it can generate interest income. Therefore very liquid securities are sometimes called *cash equivalents.*

Typical cash equivalent: US Government treasury bills

EXERCISE 1 ▶
Coke's cash

For most of the exercises in Part 2, you will need to use the Coca-Cola financial statements on page 195.

Coca-Cola's Cash and Cash Equivalents

1. ☐ How much cash and cash equivalents did Coca-Cola have in 2000?

2. Is this a large or small amount compared with total sales?

   Use a ratio to help make your decision. Divide the cash and cash equivalents figure by the 2000 sales figure.

   Ratio: Cash & equivalents to sales ☐
   ❏ Large   ❏ Small

3. Do you think Coke is planning to use this cash for an acquisition?
   ❏ Yes   ❏ No

4. Look at Coca-Cola's significant accounting policies in the notes to its accounts (*note 1*). How does it describe cash equivalents?

ACCOUNTS RECEIVABLE

You already know that accounts receivable are sales that a company has made on credit. It has delivered the product to the customer but it has not collected the cash yet.

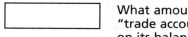

What amount of accounts receivable (Coke calls it "trade accounts receivable") did Coca-Cola have on its balance sheet on December 31 2000?

Allowances For Bad Debts

When a company sells goods on credit, it trusts customers to pay in the future. But some of those customers may default on their bills.

To prepare for some nonpayments, the company **estimates** that a proportion of its credit sales will **go bad.** This estimate shows up on the income statement as a bad debt expense.

> **EXAMPLE**
>
> | | |
> |---|---|
> | Revenues | 1000 |
> | Less bad debt expense | 50 |
> | Net revenues | 950 |

Net revenues in financial statements mean . . .

. . . revenues after allowances for bad debts

If net income changes, equity changes too. If income falls, equity will fall. The assets side of the balance sheet will need a balancing entry.

That balancing entry is a separate account called *bad debt allowance,* a contra account.

Inc. state.

Assets   L & E

Contra Accounts

A contra account is like a parasite. It lives off another account – its host. If the contra account grows, the "host" gets smaller. The bad debt allowance is attached to accounts receivable, which is its host.

Gross accts receivable or "host"	Bad debt allowance or "parasite." Contra acct.	Net accts receivable shown on bal. sheet

Journal entries for contra accounts are confusing because credits normally decrease asset accounts. But this credit increases the bad debt allowance. Because the bad debt allowance is a contra account, it reduces accounts receivable as it grows. So indirectly the credit decreases an asset account.

> **EXAMPLE**
>
> | | | | |
> |---|---|---|---|
> | **Debit** | Accounts receivable (B/S) | $1,000 | |
> | **Credit** | Revenues (I/S) | | $1,000 |
> | **Debit** | Bad debt expense (I/S) | $50 | |
> | **Credit** | Bad debt allowance | | $50 |

When a company knows exactly which customer is not going to pay, it *writes off* (removes) that particular receivable and reduces its bad debt allowance.

Debit: Bad debt allowance

Credit: Account receivable

When the company writes off an account receivable, its net accounts receivable balance does not change.

Take a look...

> Look at Coke's balance sheet and find the following two numbers:
>
> | | |
> |---|---|
> | | |
> | Gross accounts receivable | Allowance for bad debts |

EXERCISE 2 ▶

Bad debts

All About Bad Debts

1. Assume you set up a clothes store in downtown New York. You estimate that 10% of your credit sales will never be paid. In the next year you make $240,000 of credit sales.

   [_____] What is your bad debt allowance for the year?

   Fill in the journal entries:

   Debit: _____ _____

   Credit: _____ _____

2. Assume you are the financial director of Coca-Cola and you see a recession coming. You decide to increase your bad debt allowance to 5% of gross accounts receivable. Fill in the following table:

	Existing amount	+	Additional allowance	=	Ending amount
Gross accts. recv.	_____	+	_____	=	_____
Bad debt allowance	_____	+	_____	=	_____
Net accts. recv.	_____	+	_____	=	_____

3. One of your customers in Texas goes bust. They owe you $2 million. You decide write it off as a bad debt. Fill in the following table:

   Debit: _____ _____

   Credit: _____ _____

4. [_____] What is your new net accounts receivable balance?

Financial analysis tip

Account driver*

*The factors that make an account change from accounting period to accounting period. Pay attention to account drivers as you go through this book. They're important in financial analysis.

More Assets Aren't Always Better

If you give customers credit you want them to pay you as soon as possible. It costs money to "fund" those assets on your balance sheet. Good management will try to reduce the amount of money tied up in accounts receivable.

Up until now you might have thought, *The more assets a company has, the better.* But that's not usually true! Follow this reasoning:

Shareholders want the company to generate as much income as possible for their investment. If income remains constant and assets rise, the company must increase its funding to make the balance sheet balance. It has two choices:

- **It can raise debt. But then it must pay more interest expense, which reduces net income.**
- **It can raise equity. But then its net income is watered down because it's spread among more shareholders.**

In either case, the % return of the shareholders' investment will fall.

Financial Analysis

The level of accounts receivable is driven by:

- **The company's credit management;**
- **The proportion of credit sales to total sales;**
- **Selling conditions in the industry.**

Analysts use the *receivable days ratio* to compare different companies' ability to manage their accounts receivable.

$$\text{Receivable days} = \frac{\text{Average accounts receivable}}{\text{Credit sales}} \times 365$$

Note: to calculate average accounts receivable, take last year's amount, add it to this year's and divide by two. Usually you won't be able to find credit sales, so most analysts use total sales.

Receivable days tells you the average number of days between the sale and the receipt of cash. A comparatively high receivables days figure tells you a company is not chasing people who owe it money fast enough.

Not a good situation! Such a "lazy" company has to fund more accounts receivable on its balance sheet, which costs money and lowers profitability.

Less accounts receivable = fewer assets to fund = greater profitability

Put ratios in context

Analysts use ratios frequently. Remember that ratios are only meaningful *in context.* You must:

■ **Compare them to other companies in a similar business.**
■ **Look at them over time. Are they going up or down or remaining stable?**

EXERCISE 3 ▶
Coke's receivable days

What About Coca-Cola's Receivable Days Ratio?

1. [ ] Calculate Coca-Cola's receivable days using trade receivables after the allowance for bad debts. You won't find the credit sales figure so assume all the sales Coca-Cola made were on credit.

2. Suppose 3 competitors had the following receivable days ratios:

Competitor A	**35**
Competitor B	**41**
Competitor C	**42**

What does this suggest about Coke's management of its receivables?

[ ]

Your conclusions

INVENTORIES

Inventory on a company's balance sheet consists of three things:

■ **Raw materials to be used in the production process**
■ **Products in the production process that are incomplete**
■ **Finished products ready for sale**

Inventory also includes the direct costs of producing goods, such as labor, storage and freight costs.

Take a look...

Name two items in Coca-Cola's inventory figure:

1. [ ] 2. [ ]

Hint: Look in the notes to the financial statements

EXERCISE 4 ▶
Inventory detection

Coca-Cola's Inventory

Look for Coca-Cola's inventory on its balance sheet.

1. [_____] What was Coca-Cola's inventory at the end of 2000?

2. Coca-Cola started 2000 with $ _____ worth of inventory.
   Hint: look at last year's ending balance.

3. Coca-Cola took $ _____ out of the inventory account in 2000.
   Hint: look on the income statement for cost of goods sold.

4. Now use **B A S E** analysis to help you work out what CocaCola added to its inventory account during the year:

   Beginning balance in 2000   [_____]

   Additions in 2000   [_____]

   Subtractions in 2000   [_____]

   Ending balance in 2000   [_____]

Inventory records can be . . .

. . . perpetual

. . . periodic

Simple Inventory Accounting

If you make only a few sales a year, it's easy to figure out the worth of your inventory. You can keep a *perpetual inventory record,* which tracks the cost and sale price of each piece of inventory.

■ **If you are a top art dealer, you may sell only ten very expensive paintings a year. When you make a sale, you can easily identify the inventory you used to generate it.**

Complex Inventory Accounting

Tracking each item of inventory is not practical for most businesses.

■ **Coca-Cola sells millions of cases of soft drinks each year. Can you imagine tracking the manufacturing cost and sale price of each can of Coke sold?**

Companies like Coca-Cola use detective work to solve the problem of accounting for inventories. They can easily identify how much they spend increasing their inventory. It's harder for them to identify *which* items they sold *when.*

Most companies record how much stock they have in their warehouse only periodically. This is called a *periodic inventory record.*

Defining Cost of Goods Sold

Over the course of a year the prices of Coca-Cola's raw materials will probably rise due to inflation. Therefore the Coke it manufactured at the beginning of the year costs less than the Coke made at the end of the year.

If Coca-Cola doesn't track the manufacturing cost of each gallon of Coke, how will it determine the cost of the Coke it sells? It can't. Instead, Coca-Cola will *deduce* the cost of goods sold.

Three Ways to Value Inventory

There are three ways to "value" inventory:

LIFO	Last in, first out
FIFO	First in, first out
Average cost	

The following example demonstrates the three different methods.

EXAMPLE

Assume you set up a gas station in Los Angeles. Getty delivers gas to you each month. Each delivery is poured into a storage tank at the back of the station.

Over the last four months you sold 36,000 gallons of gas and took the following deliveries:

	May	June	July	August
Gallons	15,000	15,000	15,000	15,000
Price per gallon	$0.30	$0.70	$1.00	$1.10
Total invoice	$4,500	$10,500	$15,000	$16,500

Because oil prices were very volatile during the four months, the price you paid for gas rose from $0.30 to $1.10. You can't easily establish your cost of gas sold because all the deliveries were poured into the same tank at the back of your station. GAAP accounting gives you three ways to work out your cost of goods sold at the end of four months:

* **Last in First Out (LIFO)**
  This method assumes you sold the gas which was delivered last (the newest gas) first:

Delivery				COGS
15,000	$1.10 * 15,000	=		$16,500
15,000	$1.00 * 15,000	=		$15,000
6,000	$0.70 * 6,000	=		$ 4,200
36,000				**$35,700**

continued on next page

EXAMPLE: continued

* **Last in First Out (LIFO)**
  This method assumes you sold the oldest gas (the first gas delivered) first:

Delivery				COGS
15,000	$0.30 * 15,000	=		$ 4,500
15,000	$0.70 * 15,000	=		$10,500
6,000	$1.00 * 6,000	=		$ 6,000
36,000				**$12,000**

* **Average cost**
  This method uses the average cost of all the gas you bought to work out your cost of goods sold:

Delivery	COGS
15,000	$ 4,500
15,000	$10,500
15,000	$15,000
15,000	$16,500
60,000	**$46,500**

Average cost	= $46,500/60,000 =	$0.78
COGS	= $0.78 * 36,000 =	**$28,080**

Summary

LIFO	gives you the highest COGS figure but the lowest inventory figure.
FIFO	gives you the lowest COGS figure but the highest inventory figure.
Average cost	COGS and inventory figures will always fall between LIFO and FIFO.

Try the next exercise using the three different ways companies deduce their COGS and value their inventory.

EXERCISE 5 ▶
Inventory party

> Companies can choose how they report inventory

> Average cost, FIFO, or LIFO

Inventory Accounting

Assume you operate a snack stand on the beach. During July you make several purchases of Coca-Cola at the following prices.

Date	Unit price per gallon	Gallons ordered	Total cost
July 1	$2.10	300	$ 630
July 5	$3.00	200	$ 600
July 10	$4.00	350	$1,400
July 17	$4.10	100	$ 410

During the month you sell 500 gallons of Coke. You only have one refrigerator, so you can't tell how much each gallon originally cost.

At the end of the month you take a periodic inventory to help deduce your cost of goods sold. You have 450 gallons of Coke left.

What unit cost do you apply to the Coke you sold? Under U.S. GAAP, you have three choices:

Average cost method You could take the average unit cost of all the Coke you bought.

FIFO You could assume you sold the oldest Coke in the refrigerator first. *(First in first out or FIFO method of inventory valuation.)*

LIFO You could assume you sold the newest Coke in the refrigerator. *(Last in first out or LIFO method of inventory valuation.)*

1. Find the cost of goods sold for each method of inventory valuation.

   a. [＿＿＿＿＿＿] Average cost method

   b. [＿＿＿＿＿＿] FIFO method

   c. [＿＿＿＿＿＿] LIFO method

2. Which method uses the lowest cost of goods sold?
   ❑ Average cost method　　❑ FIFO　　❑ LIFO

3. Which method will give the company the highest net income?
   ❑ Average cost method　　❑ FIFO　　❑ LIFO

4. Will the amount of tax the company expenses be higher or lower using FIFO instead of the other methods?
   ❑ Higher　　❑ Lower

continued on next page

Inventory accounting, continued

5. If you compare the ratio of net income to sales for a company that uses LIFO to the ratio for a company that uses FIFO, what fact should you consider?

6. Read note 1 ("significant accounting policies") in Coca-Cola's annual report. What does it say about Coke's inventory accounting policy?

*Account
driver*

Levels of Inventory

Usually the higher a company's sales the more inventory it needs (particularly true if a company is opening up new sales units).

Management can also have an impact on the level of inventories. If a company manages its warehouses more efficiently, it can support its sales with less inventory.

Normally inventories will remain the same proportion of a company's cost of goods sold each year.

Financial Analysis

Managing inventory effectively is a big challenge for companies. Financial analysts are interested in how well – or how badly – a company is meeting the challenge. They use a ratio called *inventory days* to find out.

$$\text{Inventory days} = \frac{\text{Average inventory}}{\text{Cost of goods sold}} \times 365$$

The inventory days ratio tells you approximately how many days it takes inventory to move through a business. Generally, a comparatively low inventory days figure is better, because a faster-moving inventory means you can support the same amount of sales with less inventory assets.

Less inventory = fewer assets to fund = greater profitability

*Financial
analysis tip*

EXERCISE 6 ▶
Inventory days

Coca-Cola's Inventory Days

1. [ ] Calculate Coca-Cola's inventory days in 2000.

2. Suppose Coca-Cola's three closest competitors had inventory days ranging from 42 to 47 in 2000. What conclusions can you draw about Coke's inventory management?

[ ]

Your conclusions

PREPAID EXPENSES

When you purchase insurance you pay your premium at the beginning of the policy. In effect you prepay for the benefit of having the insurance in the future. When a company prepays for a service we call it a *prepaid expense.*

Prepaid expenses are intangible. You cannot physically touch them. Accounting treats "pre-paid" expenses as unexpired (unused) costs. Prepaid expenses go on the _____ side of the balance sheet.

PREPAID EXPENSES AND THE I/S

Prepaid expenses are linked to SG&A costs (and sometimes COGS) on the income statement.

EXAMPLE

You agree to rent an apartment in New York and pay $6,000 (2 months' rent) in advance. Your payment is a prepaid expense.

After the two months is up, you can record the "use" of your apartment on your income statement as SG&A.

How it looks on your financial statements

Income statement
Rent expense (SG&A)	-no entry-	–6,000

Balance sheet
Cash	–6,000	-no entry-
Prepaid expenses	+6,000	–6,000

May 1	July 1

Account driver

	What was the balance of Coca-Cola's prepaid expenses and other assets at the end of 2000?

Prepaid Expenses Follow SG&A

Prepaid expenses usually remain the same proportion of SG&A from year to year. For example, a portion of Coca-Cola's prepaid expenses is advertising costs which are part of SG&A. If Coke spends proportionally more on advertising, SG&A and prepaid expenses will rise.

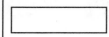

EXERCISE 7 ▶
Your new apartment

Prepaid Rent

Write out the appropriate journal entries for the following transactions:

1. You move into a new apartment. The landlord asks for $10,000 for six months' rent in advance. You reluctantly hand over a check:

   Dr _____ _____

   Cr _____   _____

2. Three months later you recalculate your balance sheet. How do you account for the prepaid rent that expired?

   Dr _____ _____

   Cr _____   _____

3. Which of the following assets are prepaid expenses?

   a. ❏ Yes ❏ No Goods waiting to be sold.

   b. ❏ Yes ❏ No One rent payment for the following 12 months

   c. ❏ Yes ❏ No A payment for a bottling machine at Coca-Cola

   d. ❏ Yes ❏ No Wages paid in cash by Coca-Cola

   e. ❏ Yes ❏ No Insurance premium paid by Coke for next year.

4. [_____] How much advertising had Coke prepaid at the end of 2000? *Hint: look at note 1 in the annual report.*

OTHER CURRENT ASSETS

Those "other" accounts

Companies often combine small accounts into an 'other' category. Sometimes the company will include information about this category in the notes to the financial statements. Always check the notes in the annual report when you are unclear what an account represents.

*Financial
analysis tip*

Financial Analysis Tip

Many times you will be unable to find out what these "other" accounts really are. One technique financial analysts use is to track their proportion of sales or total assets over time.

If the account remains a stable percentage of sales, it's likely to be driven by everyday *operational activities,* like making sales. Current assets or liabilities are also more likely to be driven by operational activities.

If the account remains the same $ amount over time it is likely to be driven by a one-off event like taking out a loan.

EXERCISE 8 ▶
Recap

Recap Current Assets		
1. ❑ Yes	❑ No	Most current assets are resources that are essential to a company's operations
2. ❑ Yes	❑ No	Current assets typically become expenses or turn into cash within a year.
3. ❑ Yes	❑ No	Cash is a current asset.
4. ❑ Yes	❑ No	If a company takes out a loan it is accounted for as a current asset.
5. ❑ Yes	❑ No	The buildings a company owns are current assets.

69

2. Current Liabilities

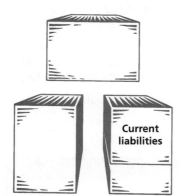

Current
liabilities

*Account
driver*

Now you're going to jump across to the other side of the balance sheet to check out the current liabilities. These are obligations that are generated in the ordinary course of a company's business and are due within one year.

ACCOUNTS PAYABLE

You already know accounts payable are bills owed to other people, usually for inventory purchased on credit. Typically these bills are interest free: the person you owe money to probably won't charge you interest on your overdue account. Therefore **accounts payable are cheap funding for you!**

Generally a higher accounts payables figure is better as you are getting more free credit. However, you must be careful not to pay your bills too late or your suppliers might stop selling to you.

Accounts payable are driven by the credit terms the company can get from its suppliers. A powerful or well-managed company will be able to get good credit terms, which means it will enjoy a higher payables balance relative to its total COGS.

A company's accounts payable are likely to remain the same proportion of cost of goods sold over time if industry practices or management doesn't change.

ACCRUED EXPENSES

Accrued expenses are the opposite of prepaid expenses. You have used services or received goods but have not yet been billed for them.

Salaries are a good example. Most people get paid in arrears. The company you work for *accrues* your wages. Do you charge interest on your unpaid salary? No! Again, this is another account that provides free funding for a company.

ACCRUED EXPENSES 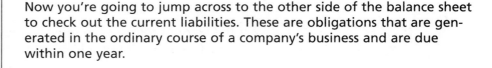 AND THE I/S

Accrued expenses are usually linked to SG&A costs on the income statement. Companies usually accrue expenses for services like utilities or labor. Some accrued expenses may be linked to COGS, for example, the accrued wages of factory workers.

<table>
<tr><td colspan="3">EXAMPLE</td></tr>
</table>

Assume you are paid $8,000 at the end of each month. Just before you get your check, the company has finished accruing your $8,000 salary expense.

How it looks on your financial statements

Income statement

Salaries (SG&A)	–8,000	-no entry-

Balance sheet

Cash	-no entry-	–8,000
Accrued expenses	+8,000	–8,000

March 30	March 31

EXERCISE 9 ▶
Free credit

Accounts Payable and Accrued Expenses

Notice how Coke lumps accounts payable and accrued expenses together on the balance sheet.

1. [＿＿＿＿] What was the balance of accounts payable and accrued expenses in 2000?

2. How does Coca-Cola break down its accounts payable and accrued expenses in the notes? *Hint: see note 4*

Name of division	Amount in $
＿＿＿＿＿＿	＿＿＿＿
＿＿＿＿＿＿	＿＿＿＿
＿＿＿＿＿＿	＿＿＿＿
＿＿＿＿＿＿	＿＿＿＿
＿＿＿＿＿＿	＿＿＿＿
＿＿＿＿＿＿	＿＿＿＿

3. [＿＿＿＿] Coca-Cola also has an account called accrued income taxes (taxes expensed on the income statement and due within one year). How much were they in 2000?

Hold On for Short-Term Debt

Short-term debt (loans due within a year or less and current maturities of long-term debt) is also a current liability. You'll learn about it later.

3. Working Capital

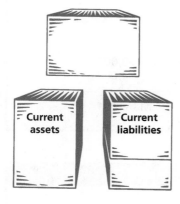

Current assets

Current liabilities

Working capital is an important analytical concept. It's the difference between current assets and current liabilities.

Working Capital	=	Current assets	–	Current liabilities

If a company's working capital is positive, its current assets are larger than its current liabilities. Some of its current assets will need financing through equity or long-term debt.

EXAMPLE

A company has the following current assets and liabilities:

Cash	110	Short-term debt	105
Receivables	150	Payables	200
Inventory	200	Accrued expenses	100
Total	460	Total	405

Working capital = 55 (460 – 405)

This company has $55 more current assets than liabilities. It has to fund these assets in some way. Therefore, it needs financing, which it can get either through debt or equity.

EXERCISE 10▶
Working capital

Calculate Working Capital

1. Which accounts are included in working capital?
   - ❑ Yes ❑ No Cash
   - ❑ Yes ❑ No Buildings, land & equipment
   - ❑ Yes ❑ No Long-term debt

2. Calculate working capital using the following balance sheet info:

Cash	53
Receivables	68
Inventory	150
Short-term debt	80
Accounts payable	54
Accrued taxes	20

Working capital =

3. A company increases its inventory. What happens to working capital?
   - ❑ Increases   ❑ Decreases   ❑ Remains the same

4. A company takes out a short-term loan. What happens to working capital?
   - ❑ Increases   ❑ Decreases   ❑ Remains the same

5. A company pays a bill with cash. What happens to working capital?
   - ❑ Increases   ❑ Decreases   ❑ Remains the same

Working capital measures risk

How Do Analysts Use Working Capital?

Analysts use working capital to measure a company's ability to pay its current bills. In other words, working capital is a test of liquidity.

If a company has more current assets than current liabilities (positive working capital), it can probably pay its current bills easily. Why? Because it can turn its short-term assets into cash within a year.

Another way to describe working capital is as a **measure of risk.** Does a company have enough liquid resources to withstand a sudden downturn? Positive working capital means the company can liquidate current assets to raise cash in an emergency.

EXERCISE 11▶
Changes in working capital

Changes in Working Capital

What will happen to a company's working capital balance if:

1. A company adds more inventory to support an increase in sales.
   ❑ Increases ❑ Decreases ❑ Remains the same

2. A company takes out a new short-term note for cash.
   ❑ Increases ❑ Decreases ❑ Remains the same

3. A company takes out a new long-term loan, which increases cash:
   ❑ Increases ❑ Decreases ❑ Remains the same

4. A company issues $150m of equity for cash:
   ❑ Increases ❑ Decreases ❑ Remains the same

5. A company sells off $200m of PP&E and uses the money to pay off its long-term debt:
   ❑ Increases ❑ Decreases ❑ Remains the same

6. A company faces strong competition. It decides to increase its receivable days by 14 days. It funds this increase in its accounts receivable with short-term debt:
   ❑ Increases ❑ Decreases ❑ Remains the same

OPERATING WORKING CAPITAL

Some financial analysts use *operating working capital* instead of working capital. Operating working capital excludes current assets and liabilities *not* driven by day-to-day operating activities.

Operating activities   Anything that helps a company carry out its day-to-day activities, such as making sales, purchasing supplies, paying bills to suppliers, and paying salaries.

Operating working capital does not include any accounts driven by investing or financing decisions.

Investing activities   Anything related to PP&E, investments in stocks and bonds, and other long-term assets.

Financing activities   Anything related to raising money through debt or equity.

Comparing Working Capital and Operating Working Capital

Analysts use operating working capital because it's a better measure of the funding needed for the company's daily activities (operating activities).

In addition, a company can't manipulate its operating activities as easily as its investing or financing activities. A company can always wait to buy that new factory; it can't wait to replace the inventory it sold.

Operating working capital   Includes only current assets and liabilities that move with operating decisions.

Working capital   Includes all current assets and liabilities.

EXAMPLE

A company has the following current assets and liabilities:

Cash	110	Short-term debt	105
Receivables	150	Payables	200
Inventory	200	Accrued expenses	100
Total	460	Total	405

Operating working capital   = $50 = (350 – 300)

Notice cash and short-term debt are not included.

As a general rule:

Operating working capital	=	Current assets – cash	–	Current liabilities – debt

Negative Operating Working Capital

Operating working capital is not always positive. Some companies can have negative operating working capital. They are companies whose current operating liabilities are greater than their current operating assets. For these lucky companies, operating working capital serves as a source of funds.

For example, magazine publishers collect subscription revenues in advance covering magazine deliveries for the next year. These advance revenues are recorded as a current liability. Receivables and inventory requirements are relatively low, resulting in a negative operating working capital figure which serves as a source of funds for the business.

EXERCISE 12▶

Coke's operating working capital

Calculate Operating Working Capital for Coca-Cola

$ in millions

1. Calculate Coca-Cola's operating working capital for 1999 and 2000.

	1999	2000
Sales		
Accounts receivable		
Inventories		
Prepaid expenses		
Accounts payable		
Accrued taxes		
Operating working capital		
Op. w. cap. as % of sales		

Estimating the Level of Operating Working Capital

Three key drivers of a company's operating working capital:

1. Its type of business and product

Account driver

- **Does the company manufacture products? Manufacturing companies usually have a high operating working capital/sales ratio due to large amounts of inventory.**

- **How long does it take for the company to manufacture the product? The longer it takes to manufacture a product the higher the level of inventories.**

- **Does the company provide a service? Service companies usually have a relatively low operating working capital/sales figure due to low inventory balances.**

2. Industry practices and management decisions

■ **Do customers pay cash or take credit? Higher credit sales mean higher accounts receivable.**

■ **Can the company buy on credit or does it have to pay cash? More credit purchases mean higher accounts payable and accrued expenses.**

■ **Does the management like to hold large stocks of inventory?**

■ **How much power does the company have over its customers and suppliers? More power means you are paid earlier by your customers, but you pay your suppliers later.**

3. Accounting practices

■ **Does the company use LIFO or FIFO to account for its inventory? When prices are rising FIFO produces a higher inventory figure as you use your old inventory first.**

EXERCISE 13 ▶
One last time

Coke's Operating Working Capital, Again

Use your solution to Exercise 12 to answer the following questions.

1. Why has Coca-Cola's operating working capital changed as a % of sales?

2. Will Coca-Cola's working capital increase or decrease?
   ❏ Increase   ❏ Decrease

3. What does Coca-Cola's operating working capital balance suggest about its power over its suppliers?

Deal #5

_____
your name

_____
value of completed deal

SCORE PAD

1. _____

2. _____

3. _____

4. _____

5. _____

6. _____

7. _____

8. _____

9. _____

10. _____

Total

Close the Deal #5

Get another tombstone by earning **$100,000** If you make less than $100,000, review the material before you go on.

1. Calculate operating working capital and working capital for the following company:

CloseShave, 2000

Income taxes payable	319.4
Cash and equivalents	81.6
Accounts payable	1,609.8
Short-term investments	1.6
Loans payable (short-term)	634.7
Current portion of LTD	26.5
Accounts receivable	2,290.8
Inventories	1,267.6
Prepaid expenses	199.3
Other current assets	246.8

[ ]	[ ]
Operating working capital	*Working capital*

2. What is the key difference between operating working capital and working capital? Why would you use operating working capital?

[   ]

3. A company uses LIFO to calculate its ending inventory at the end of the year. If it used FIFO would its inventory be higher or lower? Assume prices are rising.   ❑ higher   ❑ lower

4. If a company pays $10m cash for insurance a month before the policy starts what would the journal entries be?

Dr _____ _____

Cr _____   _____

5. [   ] If a company starts paying its bills later, which account on the balance sheet will rise?

6. [   ] If a company never made any sales on credit, what account would be missing from their balance sheet?

continued on next page

Close the Deal #5, continued

7. Which method of inventory accounting will yield a larger positive operating working capital? Assume prices are rising.

❑ LIFO   ❑ FIFO

8. Which of the following accounts should **not** be included in an operating working capital calculation? Explain each answer.

❑ No   Account receivable _____

_____

❑ No   Marketable securities which are cash equivalents _____

_____

❑ No   Accrued expenses _____

_____

❑ No   Inventories _____

_____

❑ No   Other current liabilities related to new debt financing

_____

❑ No   Accounts payable _____

_____

9. A company makes $100,000 of credit sales and estimates 5% of its customers won't pay. How does it account for the sales?

Dr   _____   _____

Cr   _____   _____

How does it account for its estimate for bad debts?

Dr   _____   _____

Cr   _____   _____

10. Suppose you run a large pharmaceutical company. If the US government deregulated the healthcare industry resulting in greater competition in your business sector, what is likely to happen to your accounts receivable?

❑ Rise   ❑ Fall   ❑ Remain the same

4. Debt

EXERCISE 14 ▶

Debt due within 12 months

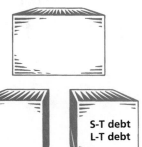

S-T debt
L-T debt

SHORT-TERM DEBT

Debt that is borrowed for periods of less than one year is a current liability.

Current Debt Liabilities

1. Name the two current debt accounts on Coca-Cola's balance sheet:

   a. _____

   b. _____

2. When will Coca-Cola have to pay this debt back?

   _____

   _____

3. Look at the notes under short term borrowings and credit arrangements. What do Coca-Cola's loans and notes payable (corporate bonds) consist of? *Hint: Look in Note 5.*

Current Portion of Long-Term Debt

"Current portion of LTD" is exactly what it says it is – the long-term debt you have to pay back in the next twelve months. So Coca-Cola has to pay back $21m worth of long-term debt between December 31, 2000 and December 31, 2001.

This $21m was taken from last year's long-term debt account in the long-term liabilities section of the balance sheet.

> **EXAMPLE**
>
> You are Coca-Cola's chief financial officer and you take out a $100 m loan. You must pay the loan off over five years starting in the middle of year two:
>
> | End of ... | Year 1 | Year 2 | Year 3 | Year 4 | Year 5 | Year 6 |
> |---|---|---|---|---|---|---|
> | Current maturity of LT debt | 20 | 20 | 20 | 20 | 20 | 0 |
> | Long-term debt | 80 | 60 | 40 | 20 | 0 | 0 |
> | Total debt outstanding | 100 | 80 | 60 | 40 | 20 | 0 |

LONG-TERM DEBT

Long-term debt is debt originally raised for periods longer than one year.

EXERCISE 15▶
Long-term debt

Coca-Cola's Long-Term Debt

- In 2000 Coca-Cola's total long-term debt amounted to $856m.

- $21m of this debt was due in the next twelve months.

- Assume that company issues no more long-term debt in 2001 and answer the following questions:
  Hint: Read note 6 in the financial statements

1. [ ] What will be Coca-Cola's current maturity of long-term debt in 2001?

2. [ ] What will be Coca-Cola's long-term debt on its 2001 balance sheet?

A key part of a financial analyst's job in an investment bank is to help clients get funding at the lowest cost possible. One of the ways a company can fund itself is by using **debt.**

Unlike equity, debt funding must be paid back. The easiest way to think about debt is as a series of cash flows.

Financial analysis tip

Cash flows

Borrowers **receive** cash   when they raise money;

Borrows **pay out** cash   either as interest or principal during the life of the loan.

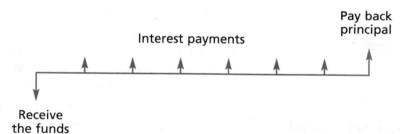

Pay back principal

Interest payments

Receive the funds

Principal   The amount of the loan. It's the money you agree to pay back when the loan is due. It is also known as the face amount of the loan.

Debt capital is riskier than equity . . .

. . . from the company's point of view

Companies are legally obliged to pay the interest and principal due to debt holders. A company is not legally obliged to pay dividends to equity holders. Therefore funding with debt capital is riskier to the company than funding with equity capital.

You usually see the total long-term debt outstanding on a company's balance sheet. You have to look in the notes to the financial statements to find when and how much the company raised at one particular time. Remember, the current portion of long-term debt is recorded in current liabilities.

EXERCISE 16 ▶
Debt close-up

Coca-Cola's Long-Term Debt in Detail

Look at Coca-Cola's balance sheet.

1. [ ] How much of Coca-Cola's long-term debt comes due in 2001?

2. Which debt 'issues' come due in 2001?

[ ]

Hint: look in the notes to the financial statements

3. How much long-term debt does Coca-Cola have to pay back in the following years?   Hint: look in the notes

	2001	2002	2003	2004	2005
LT Debt to be repaid					

4. If Coca-Cola raised $400m of debt in the financial markets, what would be the new balances of assets, liabilities and equity?

Assets [ ]   **Liabilities** [ ]

Equity [ ]

5. If Coca-Cola repaid $300m of its existing debt early, what would be the new balances of assets, liabilities and equity?

Assets [ ]   **Liabilities** [ ]

Equity [ ]

5. Tangible Long-Term Assets

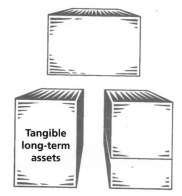

Tangible long-term assets

Long-term assets are expected to be valuable to the entity for **_longer than one year._** There are two types of long-term assets:

- **Those you can physically touch, called _tangible assets._**
- **Those you cannot see or feel, or _intangible assets._**

PP&E

Tangible long-term assets are physical **resources** that the entity owns. They include buildings, machinery, land, cars, office equipment, etc. They are also known as **property, plant and equipment** (sometimes _fixed assets_).

Take a look...

> Look at Coca-Cola's annual report. List the tangible assets (Property, Plant & Equipment) on its balance sheet:
>
> 1. _____
>
> 2. _____
>
> 3. _____
>
> 4. _____
>
> Notice the category called _buildings and improvements._ This records the original cost of buildings bought by Coca-Cola and the cost of improvements to them.

Recording PP&E on the balance sheet

You record PP&E (fixed assets) on the balance sheet at their original cost. You add to this all the costs involved in getting the asset ready for its intended use. You do not record PP&E at its market value.

EXERCISE 17▶
Watch those legal fees

Recording the Full Cost of Equipment

Assume Coca-Cola buys a new bottling machine for $300,000. It spends $3,000 in legal fees to write a contract with the manufacturer. It is charged a $10,000 installation fee and a $1,000 transportation charge. At what cost would the bottling machine be recorded on Coca-Cola's balance sheet?

PP&E and fixed assets: two names for the same thing

Terms you should know	
Property, Plant & Equipment	All the buildings, factories, warehouses, land, and equipment a company owns combined into one account. Abbreviated PP&E or PPE.
Capital expenditure	Additions to the property, plant and equipment account. Abbreviated CAPEX.
Sales of fixed assets	Reductions in PP&E.
Gross PP&E	Original cost of the assets
Net PP&E	Gross PP&E – accumulated depreciation

DEPRECIATION

How to Recognize Wear and Tear on Assets

Most assets fall in value over time. They get "used up." This is true of most office buildings if they are not renovated on a regular basis, and it's especially true of machinery.

Apart from land, most long-term tangible assets lose their value over time unless more money is spent on them. An exception is assets that become valuable to collectors. For example, a building's design or location might suddenly become "classic" or very fashionable. But accounting recognizes only the historical cost of an asset, not its market value.

Depreciation records wear and tear

Accounting records the gradual loss of an asset's usefulness in an account called *accumulated depreciation.*

Original cost of PP&E	Original purchase cost of asset
− Accumulated Depreciation	Total value used up so far
= Net PP&E	Total value remaining

Another contra account, like bad debt allowance

Accumulated depreciation is a *contra asset account,* which is a negative account. You can think of it as a parasite to its host account, PP&E. When accumulated depreciation goes up, Net PP&E must fall.

Net PP&E is simply gross PP&E less accumulated depreciation. All three accounts appear on the balance sheet, but Net PP&E is the only account which is added to total assets.

EXAMPLE

Assume you buy a new car for $25,000. You assume it will last five years and will have no salvage value. Here's your balance sheet when you buy the car:

PP&E (car)	$25,000
Accum. depr.	$0
Net PP&E	$25,000

After 2½ years, your balance sheet looks like this:

PP&E (car)	$25,000
Accum. depr.	($12,500)
Net PP&E	$12,500

After 5 years, your balance sheet looks like this:

PP&E (car)	$25,000
Accum. depr.	($25,000)
Net PP&E	$0

Financial analysis tip

You can tell how old a company's fixed assets are by dividing its accumulated depreciation by its PP&E (gross fixed assets).

The larger this number is, the older the company's fixed assets.

Analyzing PP&E

1. You are advising a paper manufacturing company which wants to acquire a logging mill. After a few days of research you find two suitable targets. One of your client's key requirements is to purchase the company with the most up-to-date plant and equipment. Which company would you recommend to your client?

   ❑ Watermill Logging Inc

Gross plant and equipment	5,000,000
Accumulated depreciation	(1,000,000)
Net plant and equipment	4,000,000

   ❑ Oregon Loggers Inc

Gross plant and equipment	5,000,000
Accumulated depreciation	(4,000,000)
Net plant and equipment	1,000,000

2. Does Coca-Cola have relatively old or new property plant and equipment in 2000 compared to its competitor below?

   ❑ Old   ❑ New

	PepsiCo
Gross plant and equipment	9,539
Accumulated depreciation	(4,101)
Net plant and equipment	5,438

	PepsiCo	Coke
$\dfrac{\text{Accumulated depreciation}}{\text{Gross PP\&E}}$		

How to Account for Depreciation

When you add depreciation to the balance sheet . . .

> . . .Your **accumulated depreciation rises...**
>> . . .Your **total assets fall . . .**
>>> . . .And your balance sheet **no longer balances.**

To bring the balance sheet back into balance, you record depreciation on the income statement as an expense so that. . .

> . . .Your **net income falls. . .**
>> . . .Your **retained earnings fall. . .**
>>> . . .And your balance sheet **balances.**

Here's how it looks as a journal entry:

Debit	Depreciation expense	*(I/S)*
Credit	Accum. depreciation	*(B/S)*

Take a look...

	What was Coca-Cola's depreciation expense in 2000? *Hint: look in the Selected Financial Data section of Coca-Cola's annual report under Balance Sheet Data*
	What was Coca-Cola's gross PP&E in 2000? *Hint: look on the Balance Sheet*
	What was Coca-Cola's accumulated depreciation in 2000?
	What was Coca-Cola's Net PP&E in 2000?

Calculating Depreciation

When a company buys a new fixed asset, it estimates how many years of useful life the asset will have and its expected salvage value at the end of its life.

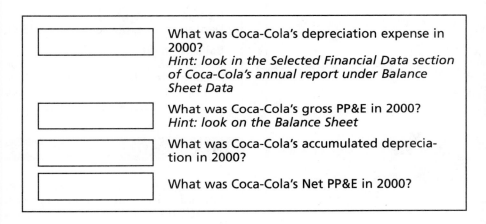

$$
\begin{array}{r}
\text{Original cost of asset} \\
-\quad \underline{\text{Estimated salvage value}} \\
=\quad \text{Total depreciation}
\end{array}
$$

Each year the company will expense part of the asset's total depreciation. It has a choice of two ways to calculate its yearly depreciation expense:

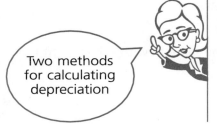
Two methods for calculating depreciation

- **Straight-line depreciation**
- **Accelerated depreciation**

Straight-Line Depreciation in Three Easy Steps

1. **Subtract**   your estimate of the salvage value from the asset's original cost to get your total depreciation.

2. **Estimate**   how many years you expect the asset to last.

3. **Divide**   your total depreciation by the number of years you expect the asset to last.

  Result: the yearly depreciation expense over the life of the asset.

When you have fully depreciated the asset, only the salvage value will be left on the balance sheet.

EXAMPLE

Black Diamond Ski Stores, Inc., purchased a delivery truck which cost $50,000. Management expected the truck to last three years and have a residual value of $5,000.

	Year 1	Year 2	Year 3	Year 4
Income statement				
Depreciation expense	15,000	15,000	15,000	0
Balance sheet				
Gross PP&E	50,000	50,000	50,000	50,000
Accumulated depreciation	15,000	30,000	45,000	45,000
Net PP&E	35,000	20,000	5,000	5,000

EXERCISE 18▶
The bottling machine

Calculate Straight-Line Depreciation

Assume that Coca-Cola bought a new bottling machine for $314,000 (including installation and setup costs). Now assume that Coca-Cola expects the machine to last for five years and have a salvage value of $10,000 at the end of that time.

Calculate how much Coca-Cola would depreciate this asset each year, using straight-line depreciation.

Accelerated depreciation

Accelerated depreciation means:

1. *Higher* depreciation in the early years;

2. *Lower* depreciation in the later years.

3. The total depreciation expense is the same as with the straight line method but the *timing* is different.

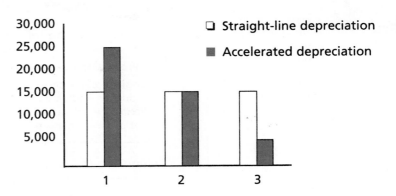

Straight-line vs. accelerated depreciation

EXAMPLE

Assume Black Diamond decided to use accelerated depreciation. See the graph above.

	Year 1	Year 2	Year 3	Year 4
Income statement				
Depreciation expense	25,000	15,000	5,000	0
Balance sheet				
Gross PP&E	50,000	50,000	50,000	50,000
Accumulated depreciation	25,000	40,000	45,000	45,000
Net PP&E	25,000	10,000	5,000	5,000

Look at Coca-Cola's annual report.

What method of depreciating assets does Coca-Cola typically use?
❑ Straight line   ❑ Accelerated

Hint: look in the note to the accounts headed "Accounting Policies."

Depreciation and the Income Statement

Where is depreciation expense recorded on the income statement?

Answer: It depends on the type of fixed assets you are depreciating.

Production assets:	Add depreciation to **COGS**
Non-production assets:	Add depreciation to **SG&A**

EXERCISE 19▶
Depreciation workout

Depreciation

A company had the following assets in its accounts:

Production fixed assets		Non-production fixed assets	
Original cost of production equipment	500,000	Headquarters building	50,000
Accum. depreciation	150,000	Accum. depreciation	20,000
Net production assets	350,000	Net non production assets	30,000

Assume the company uses straight-line depreciation.

1. The company is depreciating the headquarters building by $5,000 each year. The expected residual value of the building is $10,000. How long did the company estimate the building will last?

2. How much depreciation will the company expense for its headquarters building next year? Where would you find it on the income statement?

3. If the production equipment had no salvage value and an estimated life of ten years, how many years has the company owned the equipment?

4. How much depreciation expense will the company include in its COGS next year?

5. What was the company's total depreciation expense this year?

6. Does the net asset value necessarily reflect the market value of a company's fixed assets?　❏ Yes　❏ No

Selling Non-Current Assets

Although companies buy fixed assets to hold for long periods, they may want to sell them before their original cost is fully depreciated.

When you sell an asset, you must remove from the balance sheet **both** the accumulated depreciation and the gross PP&E assigned to the asset.

When you sell an asset you typically receive cash. If the cash you receive does not equal the *carrying value* (*net PP&E value*) on your balance sheet, the balance sheet won't balance after you record the transaction. Therefore:

Carrying value = Net PP&E value

- **If the cash you receive is lower than the asset's carrying value, record ("expense") a *loss* on the income statement.**
- **If the cash you receive is higher than the asset's carrying value, record a *gain* on the income statement.**

EXAMPLE

Assume you own a van that originally cost $10,000. So far, you have $3,500 of accumulated depreciation recorded against it, making its carrying value, also known as *book value,* $6,500.

Suppose you decide to sell it.

1. If you sell it for $5,000,
   - Cash increases by $5,000, and
   - Net PP&E falls by $6,500.
   - So total assets fall by $1,500.

   A < L&E. Your balance sheet doesn't balance!

   To make it balance, record a loss of $1,500 on the income statement in *Other expenses.*

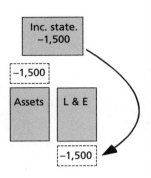

   Your journal entries would look like this:

Dr	Cash (B/S)	$5,000	
Dr	Acc depn (B/S)	$3,500	
Dr	Other expenses (I/S)	$1,500	
Cr	Gross PP&E (B/S)		$10,000

2. If you sell the asset for $9,000:
   - Cash increases by $9,000
   - Net PP&E decreases by $6,500
   - So total assets rise by $2,500.

   A > L&E. Your balance sheet doesn't balance!

   To make it balance, record a gain of $2,500 on the income statement in *Other income.*

   Your journal entries would look like this:

Dr	Cash (B/S)	$9,000	
Dr	Acc depn (B/S)	$3,500	
Cr	Gross PP&E (B/S)		$10,000
Cr	Gain on sale (I/S)		$ 2,500

EXERCISE 20 ▶

That bottling machine again

Coco-Cola's Fixed Assets

1. In 2001 Coca-Cola sold a bottling machine that originally cost $500. Its accumulated depreciation was $200. If it was sold for no gain or loss, show the journal entries.

   Dr _____ _____

   Dr _____ _____

   Cr _____ _____

2. If the same asset is sold for a $200 gain, how would you record the sale?

   Dr _____ _____

   Dr _____ _____

   Cr _____ _____

   Cr _____ _____

3. If the asset is sold for a $150 loss, how would you record it?

   Dr _____ _____

   Dr _____ _____

   Dr _____ _____

   Cr _____ _____

4. If an asset is sold at a loss, is it a loss of cash or a paper loss?

   ❏ Cash   ❏ Paper

5. Coca-Cola's balance sheet on December 31, 2000:

Total property, plant, and equipment	$6,614
Accumulated depreciation	$2,446
Net property, plant and equipment	$4,168

   Assume that in 2001 Coca-Cola sold property, plant and equipment (PP&E) that originally cost $300m and had $100m of accumulated depreciation allocated to it.

   Assume that Coca-Cola also bought $1,000m worth of new PP&E and depreciated its existing PP&E by $500m. Use the following table to calculate Coca-Cola's ending Net PP&E balance in 2001.

	Gross PP&E	Acc depr	Net PP&E
Beginning balance			
Additions			
Subtractions			
Ending balance			

6. Intangible Long-Term Assets

Financial analysis tip

Intangible assets are resources you cannot touch. Intangible assets are split into two main categories:

- **Goodwill**
- **Other intangible assets**

GOODWILL

When one company buys another company, it is buying more than just assets on a balance sheet. It's also buying some intangibles, like the quality of the employees and client base, its reputation, or its brand name.

You don't normally record these intangibles on a balance sheet because they are difficult to measure. But when you buy another company, you record these valuable intangibles on your balance sheet as *goodwill.* The purchase price includes these intangibles. If PepsiCo bought Coca-Cola, part of the purchase price would include Coke's brand name and reputation.

> **EXAMPLE**
>
> Suppose you buy a company's equity for $100 cash. On their balance sheet the equity has a book value of $30.
>
> | What you paid | What you got | Difference |
> |:---:|:---:|:---:|
> | $100 cash | $30 equity | $70 |
>
> The difference between what you paid and what you got is goodwill.
>
> *Note: Complex issues cluster around this topic. For more details, look into consolidation accounting.*

EXERCISE 21▶
Goodwill

Goodwill

1. [ ] You buy a company for $400m. It has $500m of assets and $300m of liabilities. How much is your goodwill?

2. What does goodwill represent?

[   ]

AMORTIZATION

Tangible assets are depreciated. The depreciation of *intangible* assets is called *amortization.*

- **Intangible assets with an indefinite life are not amortized, for example, goodwill.**
- **Intangible assets with a finite life are amortized straight line over their life, for example, patents.**
- **Intangibles have no salvage value.**

Like depreciation, amortization is expensed (recorded) on the income statement and accumulated on the balance sheet. Amortization is incorporated into SG&A on the income statement.

However, unlike depreciation, you are unlikely to see an account called *Accumulated amortization.* On the balance sheet, finite intangible assets are usually shown after accumulated amortization has been subtracted

EXERCISE 22▶
Goodwill extravaganza

More Goodwill

1. What is the amount of Coca-Cola's goodwill and other assets in 2000?

   Goodwill and other assets _____

2. What is Coca-Cola's principal method of amortization for intangible assets? ❏ Straight line ❏ Accelerated
   Hint: check note 1

3. [   ] What was Coke's accumulated amortization balance on December 31, 2000? *Hint: check note 1*

4. Assume Coca-Cola bought a patent and recorded a $500m intangible asset. Coca-Cola decided to amortize the patent over ten years. Fill in the following table:

End of	Year 1	Year 2	Year 3	Year 4	Year 5
Amortization expense on the income statement					
Accumulated amortization					
Balance of intangibles on the balance sheet					

5. Is amortization a cash expense? ❏ Yes ❏ No

6. [   ] What was Coca-Cola's depreciation in 2000? *Hint: look in the selected financial data section*

7. [   ] What was the amount of Coca-Cola's depreciation and amortization in 2000? Hint: look in the consolidated statement of cash flows, page 53 in the booklet.

8. [   ] Using your answers to the last two questions, find Coca-Cola's amortization expense in 2000.

OTHER INTANGIBLE ASSETS

Other intangibles include:

Other Intangibles
Patents
Franchises
Licenses

Intangible assets like franchises and patents are included on the balance sheet only when they are bought from an external entity, not if they are developed internally.

According to some valuation sources its "Coca-Cola" brand's real value is over $39 billion. However, Coca-Cola's total assets on its balance sheet are only $21 billion. Why the discrepancy? Because the Coca-Cola brand has never been properly measured.

When you buy another company's trademark you are also measuring its value so you will record the purchase on your balance sheet as an intangible asset.

Intangibles are recorded on the balance sheet only when they are purchased from another entity.

EXERCISE 23▶

What's in a name?

Coca-Cola's Brand Name

1. Coca-Cola's brand name is estimated to be the most valuable asset the company has. Why is it not shown on the balance sheet?

2. If PepsiCo bought the Coca-Cola brand name for $45 billion in cash how would it account for the purchase?

   Dr _____   _____

   Cr _____   _____

7. Investments: More Intangibles

*Financial
analysis tip*

*Account
driver*

Investments on the Balance Sheet

When you buy securities in the financial markets, you are purchasing an interest in another entity which is valuable to you. You hope your purchase will appreciate in value and pay a return.

When a company purchases debt securities like loans or bonds from another entity, it records the purchase as an **investment** on its balance sheet. If you are accounting for shares in another company and you have a controlling interest (*this usually means owning more than 50%*) you **consolidate** (*combine*) your accounts with the other company. If you don't own a controlling interest, you must account for the shares as **investments** on your balance sheet.

Investments Where You Own A Controlling Interest

You may have noticed the heading at the top of Coca-Cola's balance sheet, "The Coca-Cola Company and its subsidiaries." This tells you you're looking at a **consolidated balance sheet.** Coca-Cola's accountants have combined all the entities in which Coca-Cola has a **controlling interest** (*more than 50%*).

What does Note 1 say about Coca-Cola's consolidation policy?

The amount of investments on a company's balance sheet will depend on the company's strategy. If a company's strategy is to own stakes in other entities, it will have a large amount of investments on its balance sheet.

A good way to understand whether owning investments is part of a company's long-term strategy is to track their proportion of total assets over time.

EXERCISE 24 ▶
Equity, cost, or other?

Investments

1. Coca-Cola's brand name is estimated to be the most valuable asset the company has. Why is it not shown on the balance sheet?

2. What amount of Coca-Cola's investments are recorded using the cost method in 2000?

3. What is the amount of Coca-Cola's marketable securities and other assets in 2000?

Other assets

In many financial statements you will find "mystery" accounts. You can't easily understand what they represent. Don't panic! You must learn to deal with this ambiguity.

Deal #6

_____
your name

_____
value of completed deal

SCORE PAD

1. _____

2. _____

3. _____

4. _____

5. _____

6. _____

Total

Close the Deal #6

You must make $50,000 to earn this tombstone. If you make less than $50,000, review the material before you go on.

1. What is the difference between tangible and intangible fixed assets?

2. If Coca-Cola bought a building for $1,000,000, spent $50,000 on redecorating before it moved in, and paid its surveyor $5,000 to report on the building, all for cash, how would it account for the purchase of this building?

3. Assume Coca-Cola builds a new bottling plant. The plant cost $550,000 to build. Coca-Cola expects the building to last fifteen years. It also expects to be able to sell the building for $50,000 at the end of its useful life. It paid a lawyer $10,000 to draw up the contract to build the building.

   Fill in the following table setting out the building's net PP&E on Coca-Cola's accounts and its depreciation expense each year. Assume Coca-Cola uses straight-line depreciation. Show your figures in '000's.

End of	2001	2002	2003	2004	2005
Original cost of building	_____	_____	_____	_____	_____
Accumulated depreciation	_____	_____	_____	_____	_____
Net PP&E of building	_____	_____	_____	_____	_____
Depreciation expense	_____	_____	_____	_____	_____

4. [_____] Where would the bottling plant's depreciation expense be recorded on Coke's income statement?

Close the Deal #6 continued

5. You have a client who is looking at purchasing a transportation company. You look at the company's balance sheet and see that their trucks originally cost $5,000,000. The company had accumulated depreciation related to its trucks of $4,500,000. What advice would you give to your client?

6. You are the CEO of Coca-Cola. You decide to sell two buildings:

21 Park Street, Atlanta

You originally bought this building for $1,500,000. Since you bought the building you have accumulated $1,000,000 of depreciation against it. You agreed to sell the building for $600,000 cash.

Olympic Towers, 100 Center Boulevard, Atlanta

You originally bought this building for $12,000,000. Since you bought the building you have expensed $10,000,000 of depreciation against it. You agreed to sell the building for $1,000,000 cash.

Write the journal entries for these transactions:

8. Other Long-Term Liabilities

More mystery accounts

Other long-term *(non-current)* **liabilities** could include:

Deferred taxes
Pension obligations for the company's employees

The accounting for pension obligations is complex. It's not covered here.

Reminder: When you are not sure what an account is:

1. Look in the notes to the accounts to get more information

2. See if the account is related to other accounts. For example you might want to see if it stays the same percentage of total assets or sales each year.

9. Equity

Equity is the difference between assets and liabilities. It represents the company owners' claim against the assets. Remember these points about equity:

Equity reminders

- Claims against a company's assets by its equity holders are considered *after* its debt holders' claims·

- Paid-in capital is never "repaid" while the company is operating.

- Holders of equity are entitled to receive dividends. A company does not have to pay dividends.

COMMON STOCK AND APIC

A company raises new equity by selling shares. Most share certificates are issued with a specific amount printed on them (the *par value*). The total amount of par value on the shares a company has issued is recorded as *common stock* on the balance sheet.

If the company sells the shares for more than their par value, the difference is recorded as *additional paid-in capital (APIC),* or *capital surplus.*

EXAMPLE

Suppose a company issued 2m new shares. Each new share had a par value of $1 but was sold for $50. Here are the journal entries:

Dr	Cash	$100m = ($50 * 2m)
Cr	Common stock	$2m = ($2m * $1)
Cr	APIC	$98m = ($100m − $2m)

Take a look...

Look at Coca-Cola's balance sheet to find information about its shares:

	What is the par value of each Coca-Cola share?

Understand these definitions before you try Exercise 27.

Number of **issued** shares	= number of shares sold since incorporation
Number of **outstanding** shares	= shares owned by other entities

EXERCISE 25 ▶
Coke's shares

Shares

1. If Coca-Cola issued 100 new shares and sold them on Wall Street for $60 cash each with a par value of $0.25, what would you record in Coca-Cola's accounts? *Hint: you must make three entries.*

   _____

   _____

   _____

2. [ ] How many shares did Coca-Cola issue in 2000? *Hint: 2000 issued shares – 1999 issued shares*

3. [ ] What is the total number of shares that Coca-Cola has ever issued?

When a company buys back its own stock

TREASURY STOCK

Once a company has sold shares, it can buy them back at a later date. When a company buys back its shares, it records the "repurchase" in an account called *treasury stock:*

- **Enter into the treasury stock account the total price you paid to buy back the shares.**
- **Common stock or additional paid-in capital does not change.**

The treasury stock account is a **contra account** to all the company's equity accounts. Remember how accumulated depreciation is a parasite on gross property, plant and equipment? Treasury stock is a parasite on a company's equity accounts.

> **Shares outstanding** = shares issued – the number of repurchased shares

EXAMPLE

CyberTech, a software company, wanted to reduce the amount of total equity on its balance sheet. It decided to use excess cash to buy back 2m of its own shares for $5 each.

    Dr   Treasury stock $10m = (2m * $5)
    Cr   Cash $10m

At the end of the transaction, CyberTech's total assets and shareholders' equity had both fallen by $10m.

Take a look...

Look at Coca-Cola's annual report.

1. [ ] What was the balance of Coca-Cola's treasury stock in 2000?

2. [ ] Calculate the number of Coca-Cola's outstanding shares as of December 31, 2000.

RETAINED EARNINGS

Retained earnings are previous years' income that is kept in the business. Coca-Cola calls its retained earnings account "reinvested earnings."

The management of a company chooses the amount of dividends to pay out of retained earnings. Normally the amount of dividends is related to the business' profitability.

The payout ratio

Financial analysis tip

$$\text{Payout ratio} = \frac{\text{Dividends}}{\text{Net income}}$$

A fast-growing company will probably have a low payout ratio because it will use its earnings to help fund its future operations. A mature business is more likely to have a high payout ratio as it has less funding needs.

Dividends

1. Solve the base analysis for Coca-Cola's dividends. (Fill in the other boxes and derive dividends from those figures.)

Flows in and out of the retained earnings account

B [ ] Retained earnings, beginning of 2000

A [ ] Net income for 2000

S [ ] Dividends

E [ ] Retained earnings, end of 2000

continued on next page

EXERCISE 26▶
B A S E for dividends

EXERCISE 27▶
B A S E for dividends continued

Dividends continued

1. [ ] Calculate Coca-Cola's payout ratio for 2000.

2. [ ] If Coca-Cola's 2001 net income was $3,000m and it declared dividends of $1,200m what would be its 2001 reinvested earnings balance?

3. Look at the payout ratios of the three companies below. What do they tell you about the businesses?

Electricity Generating Co
80% payout ratio
[ ]

Joe's Clothing Stores Inc.
35% payout ratio
[ ]

Gates Software Co.
0% payout ratio
[ ]

Take a look...

OTHER EQUITY ACCOUNTS

Look at Coca-Cola's equity accounts.

Which equity accounts have you not yet examined?

■ Retained earnings　　■ Treasury stock

■ Common stock　　　　■ Capital surplus

❑ _____

Multinationals and currency differences

Accumulated other comprehensive income

You will see this account many times in ***multinational*** companies. Companies have to make adjustments for changes in currency exchange rates when they own assets abroad. Coca-Cola probably owns buildings and factories abroad. These are recorded at their original cost in foreign currency on Coca-Cola's foreign subsidiary's balance sheet.

But Coca-Cola's annual accounts are in dollar amounts. Each year when they consolidate their subsidiaries they must convert the original cost of these assets from the foreign currency into dollars. When the exchange rate changes, the original cost in dollar of the asset may rise or fall. These changes are matched by an entry into the other comprehensive income account.

To make sure **A = L + E**, you must make an adjustment. You show this adjustment in the equity accounts as an addition to other comprehensive income.

Take a look...

| | What was Coca-Cola's other comprehensive income on December 31, 2000? |

Accumulated other comprehensive income also includes unrealized gains and losses on securities.

Deal #7

_____
your name

_____
value of completed deal

Close the Deal #7

Another tombstone opportunity! You must make $90,000 to earn this tombstone. If you make less than $90,000, review the material before you go on.

1. Using the following information, decide which companies' equity investors stand the least chance of getting their money back if the business went bust. *Highest risk = 1*

Company	Total Debt	Total Equity	
New York Building Services	$300m	$200m	
Bishko SunTan Salons	$1000m	$5,000m	
Midwest Farming Inc	$75,000	$90,000	

2. If Coca-Cola issued $1,000m of new debt on January 1, 2001 what would its new total assets, liabilities and equity balances be?

Assets	Liabilities	Equity

continued on next page

SCORE PAD

1. _____

2. _____

3. _____

4. _____

5. _____

6. _____

7. _____

8. _____

9. _____

10. _____

Total

Close the Deal #7 continued

3. ❑ Yes   Can Coca-Cola's shareholders ever demand repayment
   ❑ No   of their original investment?

   ❑ Yes   Does Coca-Cola have to pay dividends?
   ❑ No

4. If Coca-Cola issued 100m new shares with a $0.25 par value for $50 cash each, what would the journal entries be?

   _____

   _____

   _____

5. What would be the new balances of common stock and capital surplus?

Common stock	**Capital surplus**

6. [_____] What was Coke's total shareholders' equity in 2000?

   [_____] What would shareholders' equity be if on January 1st, 2001 Coca-Cola bought back 4m shares at $60 each?

7. [_____] If in 2001 Coca-Cola generated $3,500m of Net Income and declared $1,500m of dividends ,what would retained earnings be on Dec. 31, 2001?

8. [_____] If Coca-Cola's net income is $2,300m and it declares dividends of $1,000m, what is its payout ratio?

9. [_____] What type of corporation will make foreign currency adjustments?

10. Which is riskier for an investor to own, a company's equity or its debt securities?   ❑ Equity   ❑ Debt securities

Income Statement Review
1. Revenues, COGS and SG&A

More About Revenues

You learned about revenues in Part 1. Now you'll look at revenues from an a financial analyst's point of view.

As a financial analyst, you will want to know what drives a company's revenues. You can start with its income statement, but because it's only a summary you'll get more detail by looking in the notes.

EXERCISE 28▶
Coke's business lines

Coca-Cola's Revenues by Operating Segment

Turn to note 18, "Operating Segments." Notice that each business line is broken down into several different accounts. The corporate segment refers to Coca-Cola's head office activities.

1. Calculate the profitability of Coca-Cola's geographic operations.

	North America	Latin America
Revenues		
Identifiable Operating assets		
Operating profit (income)		
Operating profit/revenues		
Operating profit/assets		

	Europe	Asia Pacific
Revenues		
Identifiable Operating assets		
Operating profit (income)		
Operating profit/revenues		
Operating profit/assets		

Which geographical segment had the best profitability in 2000?

COST OF GOODS SOLD (COGS) RECAP

EXERCISE 29 ▶

COGS recap

Cost of Goods Sold

You learned about cost of goods old in Part 1. Here's a quick recap:

1. Which balance sheet account is linked to COGS?

2. When is depreciation included in cost of goods sold?

3. Which other income statement account does cost of goods sold track?

4. Explain the matching of costs to revenues.

SG&A RECAP

SG&A Recap

You learned about SG&A in part 1. Here's a quick recap:

1. Name two balance sheet accounts linked to SG&A.

2. When is depreciation expense included in the SG&A line?

3. Where do you think Coca-Cola records most of its depreciation expense?
   ❑ COGS   ❑ SG&A

4. Where do you think Coca-Cola records its amortization expense?

Gross Profit and Operating Profit

Gross profit represents the sales revenue that remains after cost of goods sold including any depreciation related to production activities is taken away.

Gross profit

Revenues

− COGS

Gross profit

Operating profit (or income) tells you the profit that remains after accounting for COGS and SG&A including depreciation and amortization.

Operating profit

Revenues

− COGS

− SG&A

Operating profit

Gross Margin = Gross Profit/Sales

st costs in the COGS figure are *variable.* As sales go up, so will COGS. The gross margin ratio shows

$$\text{Gross margin} = \frac{\text{Gross profit}}{\text{Sales}}$$

you this relationship.

Gross margin is Usually driven by pricing and production efficiency.

- **If the industry becomes more competitive. . .**

- **If a company's production line becomes more efficient. . . .**

- **Customers will demand lower prices and companies will see their gross margins fall.**
- **Its gross margin should rise.**

Account driver

Gross margin

Gross Margin

1. Use the 'Selected Financial Data' section of Coca-Cola's annual report to track Coke's gross margin ratio over the last ten years:

Gross margin

1991		1996	
1992		1997	
1993		1998	
1994		1999	
1995		2000	

2. What do these ratios suggest about Coca-Cola's production efficiency over the last ten years assuming the price of Coke has not changed?

3. If a company's gross margin ratio includes most of its depreciation *(for instance, if it is largely a manufacturing company)* and it begins a large capital expenditure program, what will happen to its cost of goods sold if other production costs stay constant?

COGS will ☐ rise ☐ fall

Gross Margin = Operating Profit/Sales

$$\text{Operating margin} = \frac{\text{Operating profit}}{\text{Sales}}$$

Most costs in the SG&A figure are **fixed costs.** If sales go up, SG&A may not be affected. The operating margin ratio shows you this relationship.

Operating Margin

1. Track Coca-Cola's operating margin over the last ten years:

<u>**Operating profit**</u>
Sales

1991		1996	
1992		1997	
1993		1998	
1994		1999	
1995		2000	

2. What does this analysis tell you about Coca-Cola's operating performance over the last ten years?

3. Name two expenses that Coca-Cola includes in its SG&A number.

4. Find how much money Coca-Cola spent on advertising over the last two years. *Hint: look in note 1.*

Is this a significant expense for the company? ❑ Yes ❑ No

Financial analysis tip

INTEREST INCOME AND INTEREST EXPENSE

Interest income represents the amount of interest generated from a company's cash balances, investment in debt securities and loans made to outside entities.

Interest expense represents the amount of interest paid on a company's loans from outside entities. You can look at interest expense to estimate a company's average *cost of debt.*

$$\text{Average cost of debt} \quad = \quad \frac{\text{Total interest expense}}{\text{Average total debt}}$$

Average total debt: add last year's debt and this year's debt and divide by 2.

Beware of companies with seasonal debt funding requirements. Estimating the cost of debt by the averaging method can be misleading if a company takes on a lot of short-term debt between reporting periods.

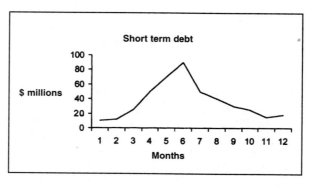

EXERCISE 32 ▶
Average cost of debt

Average Cost of Debt

1. [   ] Calculate Coca-Cola's average cost of debt in 2000. Remember to include the current maturing portion and loans and notes payable.

2. Why could the above calculation be misleading?

[   ]

3. Assuming interest rates remain constant, what will happen to a company's interest expense if it takes on more debt?

[   ]

How investment bankers add value

Interest expense is the cost of using debt to fund assets. Financial analysts help companies reduce their cost of debt by matching debt investors with debt issuers in the most efficient way.

OTHER INCOME STATEMENT ACCOUNTS

Other Expenses and Other Income

Many annual reports have accounts called *Other expenses* or *Other income.* These accounts record **unusual or infrequent income and expenses.**

Take a look...

Coke has three other expense and income accounts. What are they?
1.
2.
3.

Extraordinary Items

Extraordinary items are transactions and other events that are:

Significantly different from the company's typical business activities
AND
Not expected to recur frequently

Extraordinary items appear separately in the income statement, **net of taxes.**

Extraordinary items are shown *net of tax* (with tax taken out)

Operating profit

Interest

Taxes

Extraordinary items

Net income

Where extraordinary items appear on the Income Statement

EXERCISE 33 ▶
Extraordinary!

Financial analysis tip

Extraordinary Items

1. Are the following extraordinary items? *Hint: see test for extraordinary items on previous page*

   ❏ Yes ❏ No Loss on sale of a significant part of a company's assets

   ❏ Yes ❏ No Wages paid to a company's factory workers

   ❏ Yes ❏ No Losses as the direct result of a major casualty

   ❏ Yes ❏ No Losses resulting from prohibition under a newly enacted law or regulation

EARNINGS BEFORE INTEREST AND TAXES (EBIT)

EBIT is earnings that can be used to make interest payments. It includes all earnings and expenses **before interest expense and taxes.** A company with very large debts might have to use all of its EBIT for interest payments. It might not have any income left over for taxes or shareholders:

EBIT	The pool of available income. . .
Interest	. . .paid to debt holders
Tax	. . .paid to debt holders
Net income	. . .available to shareholders

EBIT Workout

Calculate income available to shareholders. Assume a tax rate of 50% and an interest rate of 10% of the outstanding debt balance.

	Scenario 1	Scenario 2	Scenario 3
Outstanding debt	900	450	100
EBIT	100	100	100
Interest expense			
Profit before tax			
Tax			
Net income			

2. Taxes

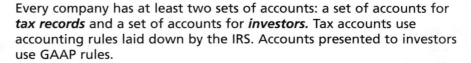

Two sets of accounting records. . .

. . .one for shareholders. . .

. . .one for the government

Every company has at least two sets of accounts: a set of accounts for **tax records** and a set of accounts for **investors.** Tax accounts use accounting rules laid down by the IRS. Accounts presented to investors use GAAP rules.

Investor accounts	Companies report their income as **fairly** as possible.
Tax accounts	Companies try to report taxable income that is as **low** as legally possible.

Many tax accounting principles are similar to GAAP rules. But when they are different, the company's taxable income will be different from its GAAP income.

One of the big differences between GAAP and tax accounting is how depreciation expense is calculated.

GAAP	Allows a variety of methods to calculate depreciation expense. A company can depreciate fixed assets using straight line or accelerated methods.
Tax accounts	Usually uses an accelerated method of accounting for depreciation

Even though a business might use straight line depreciation for GAAP purposes, it can use accelerated depreciation in its tax accounts. Most companies have to use accelerated depreciation for their tax accounts. This choice reduces their taxable income postponing the payment of taxes. It's better to pay taxes later, not earlier.

GAAP vs. Tax Accounting

Tax accounts determine how much tax you **pay** to the government each year; GAAP accounts determine how much tax you **expense** in the financial statements you show to your shareholders.

Why is it important for companies to delay their tax payments? Because they can conserve that cash and invest it in their business for the period before they hand it to the IRS.

Important! Total tax depreciation of an asset is equal to the total GAAP depreciation of the asset. The only difference is in the **timing,** or when that depreciation is recognized.

Financial analysis tip

EXAMPLE

Here's an example showing the differences between tax expensed (recorded) and tax paid. Assume the following:

- A company purchases new machinery which cost $100,000.

- The machinery is expected to last 5 years.

- The machine has no salvage value.

- The tax rate is 50%.

- Income before depreciation and taxes is $100,000 for the next 5 years.

If the company uses straight-line depreciation in its GAAP accounts and accelerated depreciation to calculate its tax payments, the yearly amount of tax it **pays** will be different from the amount it **expenses**.

Timing differences

(all figures in $000's)	Year 1	Year 2	Year 3	Year 4	Year 5	Total
GAAP Accounts						
Income	100	100	100	100	100	
Depreciation	(20)	(20)	(20)	(20)	(20)	(100)
Profit before tax	80	80	80	80	80	
Tax expensed	(40)	(40)	(40)	(40)	(40)	(200)
Tax Accounts						
Income	100	100	100	100	100	
Depreciation	(50)	(25)	(15)	(10)	0	(100)
Profit before tax	50	75	85	90	100	
Tax paid	(25)	(38)	(42)	(45)	(50)	(200)
Timing difference between tax expensed and paid	**15**	**2**	**(2)**	**(5)**	**(10)**	**0**

EXERCISE 34▶
Try your hand at taxes

Tax Accounting

1. You buy a new car for your business for $50,000. You estimate it will last five years. You expect it not to have any salvage value. Assume your profits excluding the car's depreciation expense are $50,000 each year for the next five years. Assume the tax rate is 50%. Complete a summarized income statement that you will show to your *investors*:

Year	1	2	3	4	5
Profit before tax and car depreciation	$50,000	$50,000	$50,000	$50,000	$50,000
Car depreciation expense	($10,000)	($10,000)	($10,000)	($10,000)	($10,000)
Profit before tax					
Tax at 50%					

continued on next page

Tax Accounting continued

2. However, in your tax accounts you want to use the largest depreciation deduction possible, which reduces your tax payments in the earlier years. Using a tax rate of 35%, complete the income statement you will present to the tax authorities:

Year	1	2	3	4	5
Income before tax and car depreciation	$50,000	$50,000	$50,000	$50,000	$50,000
Car depreciation in tax books	($20,000)	($15,000)	($10,000)	($5,000)	($0)
Income before tax					
Tax at 50%					

3. Now calculate the difference between the tax you paid to the tax authorities and the tax you expensed in your GAAP accounts.

Year	1	2	3	4	5
Difference between tax and GAAP amounts					

DEFERRED TAX LIABILITY

A difference between the tax a company pays and the tax it expenses in its GAAP accounts creates a problem. If you expense $20,000 of tax on the income statement and only pay out $15,000 in taxes to the government, your balance sheet will not balance. You must create an account called a **deferred tax liability:**

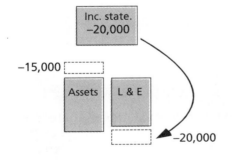

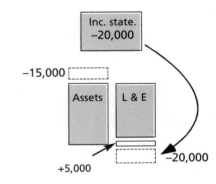

1. Balance sheet doesn't balance. It's off by $5,000.

2. A deferred tax liability of $5,000 balances the B/S

Here are the journal entries:

Debit:	Income tax expense	$20,000	
Credit:	Cash		$15,000
Credit:	Deferred tax liability		$ 5,000

In the last exercise you found the "timing difference" between GAAP and government tax reporting. Here's how GAAP deals with the timing difference in a company's financial statements:

EXAMPLE

Timing difference (amounts in thousands)	5	2.5	0	(2.5)	(5)
GAAP inc. statement					
Income tax expense	(20)	(20)	(20)	(20)	(20)
Reduction in cash	(15)	(17.5)	(20)	(22.5)	(25)
Change in def. tax liab.	5	2.5	(0)	(2.5)	(5)
GAAP balance sheet					
Deferred tax liability	5	7.5	7.5	5	0

The only accounts that change on the financial statements are income tax expense, deferred tax liability, and cash.

The deferred tax liability account shows you that sometime in the future your income tax *expense* will be lower than your income tax *payment* to the IRS.

When that time comes, and your expense is lower than your payment,. . .

. . .your balance sheet won't balance. . .

. . .so you make up the difference by reducing the deferred tax liability:

Debit:	Income tax expense	$20,000	
Debit:	Deferred tax liability	$ 5,000 *(reduction in account)*	
Credit:	Cash		$ 5,000

DEFERRED TAX ASSET

When GAAP tax expenses are lower than taxes paid to the government in cash, you put the difference into an account called a *deferred tax asset,* the opposite of the deferred tax liability.

The deferred tax asset account shows you that sometime in the future your income tax *expense* will be higher than your income tax *payment* to the IRS.

Deferred tax asset and liability are not linked to each other. They show **temporary differences** related to individual events, e.g., depreciation of a particular asset. When enough time passes they are reduced to zero.

EXERCISE 35▶
Death by taxes

Deferred Taxes	
1. ☐	What was Coca-Cola's tax expense in 2000? *Hint: look in note 14 to the accounts*
2. ☐	What proportion of Coca-Cola's tax expense was current?
3. ☐	What proportion of Coca-Cola's tax expense was deferred?
4. If Coca-Cola increases its deferred tax liabilities, is it paying more tax than it expenses? ❑ Yes ❑ No	
5. If Coca-Cola creates a deferred tax asset, does it pay tax earlier or later than it expenses the tax on its GAAP accounts? ❑ Earlier ❑ Later	

Deferred tax assets and liabilities are created for many different reasons. If a company continues to add to its deferred taxes, they will probably remain the same proportion of sales over time. If a company's deferred taxes were created by a one-time transaction then they will probably fall over time.

Effective Tax Rate

The effective tax rate is calculated by dividing your income tax expense by your pre-tax income.

Account driver

$$\text{Effective tax rate} = \frac{\text{Income tax expense}}{\text{Pre-tax income}}$$

EXERCISE 36▶
The last tax exercise

Coca-Cola's Effective Tax Rate	
☐	What was Coca-Cola's effective tax rate in 2000?

Deal #8

_____
your name

_____
value of completed deal

SCORE PAD

1. _____

2. _____

3. _____

4. _____

5. _____

6. _____

7. _____

8. _____

9. _____

10. _____

Total

Close the Deal #8

Get your next tombstone by earning $90,000. If you make less than $90,000, review the material before you go on.

1. When is depreciation included in cost of goods sold?

2. Does SG&A include more fixed or more variable costs?
   ❑ More fixed costs   ❑ More variable costs

3. A company recorded the following information in its income statement:

Revenues	$100,000
COGS	$30,000
SG&A	$10,000
Other income	$1,000
Extraordinary items	$500
Interest expense	$2,000

   Calculate the company's operating margin and gross margin.

   Operating margin   **Gross margin**

4. The same company had $30,000 of debt outstanding at the beginning of the year and $20,000 at the end of the year.

   Calculate the company's average cost of debt.

5. Is depreciation a cash expense?   ❑ Yes   ❑ No

6. What are two tests for extraordinary items?

   1)

   2)

7. Assume a construction company sold its stake in a publishing business and made a gain of $10m. Their accountants advised them that the $10m should be categorized as an extraordinary item. The company's tax rate is 40%. What amount would appear on their income statement?

continued on next page

Close the Deal #8 continued

8. [_____] Who does a company prepare its tax accounts for?

9. You record a $60m tax expense in your GAAP accounts and pay $40m in taxes to the government. Show your journal entries.

[_____]

10. Name one event that creates a deferred tax liability.

[_____]

The Cash Flow Statement

In addition to preparing an income statement and balance sheet, a company must prepare a *cash flow statement*. A cash flow statement simply describes the *flows of cash* into and out of different accounts over the course of one year. The cash flow statement is like your bank statement. It shows how cash came in and went out.

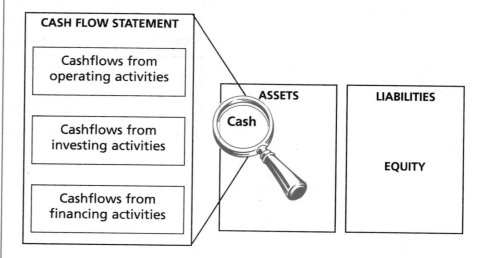

The cash flow statement is a detailed analysis of the cash account

Why financial analysts focus on cash

Cash flow statements are important to financial analysts for two reasons:·

■ **Companies can manipulate net income by changing their accounting policies (e.g., they can choose FIFO or LIFO), but they can't manipulate cash flows.**
■ **Financial analysts use cash flows in valuation and to measure cash generation when assessing a company's credit risk.**

Cash flow statements are relatively new financial statements. They were introduced due to pressure from the financial community.

Start with the cash account

To understand the cash flow statement, start with the cash account on the balance sheet. Almost every account on the balance sheet is linked to cash. Remember sources and uses of funds?

Financial analysis tip

Sources of cash
Increases in liabilities & equity
Decreases in assets

Uses of cash
Increases in assets
Decreases in liabilities & equity

Sources of cash

Debt increases	You take out a loan.	*Cash goes up.*
Accounts receivable fall	Customers pay their bills.	*Cash goes up.*

Uses of cash

Inventory rises.	You pay for raw materials.	*Cash goes down.*
Retained earnings falls	You pay dividends.	*Cash goes down.*

The Cash Flow Statement is a Summary.

Income statement:	Summary
Balance sheet:	Snapshot
Cash flow statement:	Summary

The cash flow statement summarizes the effect on cash due to changes in the balance sheet from the beginning of the period to the end.

B/S Year 1

Cash	70
Prepaid expenses	10
Marketable securities	30
Total assets	**110**
Paid-in capital	110
Total assets	**110**

Snapshot

B/S Year 2

Cash	85
Prepaid expenses	20
Marketable securities	25
Total assets	**130**
Paid-in capital	130
Total assets	**130**

Snapshot

Cash Flow Statement

Change in Prepaid expenses	(10)
Change in Marketable securities	5
Change in Paid-in capital	20
Change in cash	**15**

Snapshot

Insights from the Example

- Cash flows are either positive or negative.
  - The change in prepaid expenses increases assets, therefore:
    It's a *use of cash* (negative cash flow).
  - The change in marketable securities decreases assets, therefore:
    It's a *source of cash* (positive cash flow).
  - The change in PIC increases L&E, therefore:
    It's a *source of cash* (positive cash flow).
- The 15 change in cash is positive. Cash rises from 70 to 85.
- You get the same answer two different ways:
  - By analyzing the cash flows from each account on the cash flow statement;
  - By subtracting last year's balance sheet cash from this year's.
  - The two answers should always be equal.

EXERCISE 37▶
First cash flow statement

Your First Cash Flow Statement

Use the following two balance sheets to calculate the cash flow statement.

B/S Year 1	
Cash	90
A/R	30
Inventories	110
Total assets	**230**
Debt	100
Paid-in capital	130
Total assets	**230**

B/S Year 1	
Cash	20
A/R	50
Inventories	130
Total assets	**200**
Debt	70
Paid-in capital	130
Total assets	**200**

Cash Flow Statement

Change in A/R	
Change in inventories	
Change in debt	
Change in PIC	
Change in cash	

Net or Flow?

The example calculated the change between balance sheet accounts from the beginning to the end of a period to find the net effect on cash. Many financial statements will show you the actual cash flows in and out of an account. You can find examples in Coke's financial statements.

Look at Coke's cash flow statement and find the following examples of net changes in cash and cash inflows and outflows.

Net change		Net change in operating assets and liabilities
Cash inflow		Issuance of debt for cash
Cash outflow		Payments of debt

Non-Cash Accounts

You have just calculated your first cash flow statement. The procedure you used works for most balance sheet accounts. However, some accounts are affected by non-cash entries, so you can't just take the change in the account's balance between the beginning and end of the period:

Retained earnings	Contains non-cash expenses like depreciation, amortization, and loss on sale of assets.
	Remember that depreciation reduces net income (and therefore retained earnings) but is not a cash cost. The same is true of amortization.
Net PP&E	Accumulated depreciation is a non-cash account. When depreciation lowers the Net PP&E account, the company doesn't actually pay out cash.
Intangibles	Same issue as Net PP&E. Accumulated amortization is a non-cash account.

You'll find more non-cash accounts in your own analyses, but these are the "big three" present in almost every set of financial statements. You will learn to deal with these non-cash accounts as you continue through this section.

Three Sections

The cash flow statement has three sections. They organize the cash flows into three parts that give useful information to analysts:

Cash flows from:

Operating activities	Anything that helps a company carry out its day-to-day activities, such as making sales, purchasing supplies, paying bills to suppliers, and paying salaries.
Investing activities	Anything related to PP&E, investments in stocks and bonds, and other long-term assets.
Financing activities	Anything related to raising money through debt or equity.

CASH FROM OPERATING ACTIVITIES

Cash flow from operating activities shows you how much cash was generated by day-to-day business operations.

Cash flows from operations include:

- **Cash received from customers;**
- **Cash paid out to suppliers, employees, and tax collectors.**

In a normal profitable company, cash flow from operations should be positive. In some very fast-growing companies it could be negative.

Account driver

What About Net Income and Retained Earnings?

Isn't net income a cash flow into retained earnings? No, because net income includes some non-cash expenses and income, so it's not a true cash figure. You must adjust it to remove any non-cash expenses and income when you calculate cash flow from operations.

How to Calculate Cash Flow from Operations

Step 1: Convert net income to cash income

Cashflow from operations starts with net income. Your first step is to "clean" the non cash items from net income to get **cash income.**

To get cash income, you must add back non-cash expenses and take away non-cash income.

Examples of non-cash items include:

- **Depreciation and amortization**
- **Losses on sales of assets**
- **Equity income from accounting for investments using the equity method**

Convert net income to cash income

	Net income	Start with net income.
+	Non-cash expenses	Add non-cash expenses like depreciation and amortization. (These items appear on the income statement but don't affect cash.)
–	Non-cash income	Subtract non-cash income.

EXERCISE 38▶
Joe's London bike shop

Calculating Cash Income

Joe recently purchased a bicycle shop in London. Calculate the shop's cash income from the following information:

■ In 1995 the shop made $100,000 in net income.

■ Depreciation for the year was $30,000.

■ Amortization amounted to $10,000.

■ During the year the shop sold its van for $1,000. The van originally cost $6,000 but had $4,000 of accumulated depreciation allocated to it. In the shop's income statement you see a $1,000 loss on sale of van.

Cash income for the bicycle shop

Net income	
Non cash adjustments	
Cash income	

Step 2: Find changes in B/S accounts driven by operating activities

Operations-driven accounts usually include:

All assets and liabilities driven by the company's operating activities:

■ **Accounts receivable**
■ **Inventories**
■ **Prepaid expenses**
■ **Other current assets**

■ **Accounts payable**
■ **Accrued expenses**
■ **Other current liabilities**
■ **Deferred tax liabilities**
■ **Other long-term liabilities**

Subtract last year's account balance from this year's to find the change (the use or source of cash).

EXAMPLE

	Last year	This year	Change	Effect on cash
Inventory	5500	6200	700	−700
Deferred tax liability	500	570	70	+70

EXERCISE 39▶

Operating accounts and cashflows

Calculating Cash Income

Use the following balance sheet to calculate the cashflow from assets and liabilities driven by a company's operating activities.

Hint: Careful! Not all the accounts are included in the calculation!

Cash	100	58	☐
Inventories	203	251	☐
Receivables	301	340	☐
Prepaid expenses	28	32	☐
Net PP&E	489	480	☐
Long-term investments	323	321	☐
Total assets	1,444	1,482	

Accounts payable	289	319	☐
Short-term debt	120	150	☐
Deferred taxes	54	50	☐
Long-term debt	500	500	☐
Other liabilities	83	91	☐
Equity	398	372	☐
Total liabilities & equity	1,444	1,482	

Total change in cash from operating assets and liabilities	☐

Step 3. Account for any non-operating cash flows in cash income

Steps 1 and 2 are the important steps. You must add Step 3 only if the company has non-operating cash flows in its cash income.

EXAMPLE

Assets are sold for a profit *(amount higher than their book value)*

Suppose you own a car that cost $5,000. You have allocated $4,000 of accumulated depreciation to it and you sell it for $2,000 .

Accounting value	$1,000	Original price – accumulated depreciation
Sale price	$2,000	Cash received
Gain on sale	$1,000	Added to net income.

Important! The $1,000 gain is a cash flow, but it's not a cash flow from operating activities. It's a cash flow from an investing activity, so you take it away from cash flow from operating activities.

CASH FROM INVESTING ACTIVITIES

Part of the cash flow statement records the sources and uses of cash from a company's investing activities. Cashflows from investing activities include:

Cash inflows	Cash outflows
Sales of PP&E	Capital expenditure (CAPEX)
Sales of investments	Purchase of investments

You face two problems in finding intangible asset and PP&E cashflows.

- **The cash received from the sale of a fixed asset does not necessarily equal its original purchase price minus its accumulated depreciation. Remember that fixed assets are recorded at their original cost, and that you can have a gain or a loss on their sale.**
- **They are affected by non-cash accounts (accumulated depreciation and amortization).**

EXAMPLE

Caroline owns a chain of copy shops. She has decided to sell one of her photocopiers, which she purchased for $30,000. So far, it has accumulated depreciation of $25,000, giving a book value of $5,000. When she sells it, her net Net PP&E will fall by $5,000 (the book value) no matter what the selling price is.

- If she sells it **below book value** (at a loss of $2,000):
  Cash flow = book value minus loss on sale.
  Cash flow = $3,000 = ($5,000 – $2,000)

- If she sells it **above book value** (at a gain of $3,000):
  Cash flow = book value plus gain on sale.
  Cash flow = $8,000 = ($5,000 + $3,000)

Use BASE analysis to help find the true cashflows for intangible assets and PP&E.

EXAMPLE

Jeffrey Hair Products Inc. had the following fixed asset accounts:

All figures in 000's	1995	1996
Gross PP&E	150	180
Accumulated Depreciation	50	65
Net PP&E	100	115
Depreciation expense		35

During the year, Jeffrey sold a bottling machine that originally cost $50,000. No gain or loss was made on the sale.

Use BASE analysis to work out two numbers:

1. Capital expenditure

Gross PP&E

B	150	Beginning balance from 1995 balance sheet
A	**80**	**Capital expenditure during the year**
S	50	Original cost of assets sold during the year
E	180	Ending balance from 1996 balance sheet

The B A S E analysis works out the cash spent on fixed assets during the year. Notice that you can use B A S E analysis to solve for any part of the B A S E equation.

2. Cash flows from fixed asset sales

Accum. depreciation

B	50	Beginning balance from 1995 balance sheet
A	35	Depreciation expense during the year
S	**20**	**Accum. depn. of bottling machine (sold)**
E	65	Ending balance from 1996 balance sheet

The B A S E analysis works out the accumulated depreciation of the asset Jeffrey sold (the bottling machine).

You need this number to work out the Net PP&E value of the sold asset and the cashflow from fixed asset sales.

Net PP&E of sold asset	– loss / + gain on sale	=	Cashflow
50 – 20 = 30	No loss/gain = 0		30

Reminder

- Increases in fixed assets or investments are a use of cash;
- Decreases (sales) of fixed assets and investments are a source of cash.

EXERCISE 40 ▶
Leslie's restaurant

This is easier
than it looks!

Cashflow from Investing Activities

You invest in Leslie's new restaurant. At the end of the year, you inspect the income statement and balance sheet. Using the information below, calculate the cashflow from investing activities. Use the B A S E templates.

I/S		B/S, beg. of year	B/S, end of year
Depn	30		
		Gross PP&E	900	1,020
		Acc. depn.	100	100
		Net PP&E	800	920

Assume:

Purchase of new chairs	200
Loss on sale of used kitchen equipment	20

	Gross PP&E	Accum. depn.		Sold asset
Beg	900	100	Gross PP&E	
Add			Acc Depn.	
Sub			Book value	
End	1,020	100	Loss on sale	
			Cashflow	

Now work out the cashflows:

Capital expenditure	
Fixed asset sales	

Investing activities cashflow: positive or negative?

Companies with *negative* cash from investing activities include:

- **Manufacturing companies with lots of plant and equipment**
- **Rapidly growing companies**

Companies with *positive* or *neutral* cash from investing activities include:

- **Companies that are downsizing and selling off assets**
- **Service companies with little need for physical plant**

Financial analysis tip

129

CASH FROM FINANCING ACTIVITIES

You must also include financing cash flows in your cash flow statement. Financing cash flows include:

Cash inflows	Cash outflows
Issuance of new debt	Repayment of existing debt
Issuance of new stock	Purchase of treasury stock
	Payment of dividends

EXERCISE 41▶
Bedford Biscuits

Calculate Financing Cashflows

The Bedford Biscuit Company made the following financing decisions during the year.

- They sold 50,000 new shares for $7.10 each.
- The company took out a new loan of $200,000.
- The company reduced its short-term debt by $10,000.
- During the year, Bedford Biscuits spent $500,000 on a new biscuit cutter.
- Retained earnings at beginning of year: $123,000
- Net income during the year: $ 50,000
- Retained earnings at end of year: $150,000

Calculate the company's cash flow from **financing** activities.

Issuance of new debt

Repayment of existing debt

Issuance of new stock

Purchase of treasury stock

Payment of dividends

**Cash flow from
      financing activities**

Warning

Annual reports are summaries of many different accounts. If you try to reconcile a historical cash flow statement with changes in historical balance sheet accounts, it usually won't work!

Why? Companies don't show you everything in the annual report. Many flows in and out of accounts remain hidden. If you had the full picture then you could reconcile the balance sheet and cash flow statement.

Irreconcilable Differences

1. Use **B-A-S-E** to analyze Coca-Cola's capital surplus and common stock accounts. What is the amount of your irreconcilable difference?

B		Capital surplus and common stock, end of 1999 *Hint: look on the balance sheet*
C		Issuance of stock *See the financing section of the Cash Flow Statement*
S		Irreconcilable difference
E		Ending Capital surplus and common stock, 2000 *From the balance sheet*

When You Forecast

When you forecast a company's balance sheet and income statement you can calculate a reconcilable cash flow statement because **you** are making the assumptions of the increases or decreases of cash flows.

Your own cash flow template

All cash flow statements are different. You'll get into trouble when you try to reproduce an odd or unique cash flow statement. This book offers you a set of standard templates that will work with almost every set of financial statements.

Use them in the following exercises and in your own analysis. They work!

The templates show you which accounts are normally negative (use of funds). The parentheses in the labels will help you understand if the item is a cash inflow or outflow.

> *The next 3 exercises use the financial statements on the next page to take you though the calculation of a cash flow statement for Coca-Cola. The financial statements for 2000 were forecast by a financial analyst before the actual year-end numbers were published.*

Coca Cola's financial statements

INCOME STATEMENT	2000
Sales	20,000
COGS	(7,704)
Gross profit	12,296
SG&A	(8,000)
Operating profit	4,296
Interest income	280
Interest expense	(300)
Other income	500
income before tax	4,776
Taxes	(1,480)
Net income	3,296

BALANCE SHEET	1999	2000
Cash and cash equivalents	1,611	1,819
Marketable securities	201	73
Trade accounts receivable	1,798	1,757
Inventories	1,076	1,066
Prepaid expenses and other assets	1,794	1,905
Total current assets	6,480	6,620
Investments	6,792	5,765
Marketable securities & other	2,124	2,364
Gross PP&E	6,471	6,614
Accumulated Depreciation	2,204	2,446
Net PP&E	4,267	4,168
Goodwill and other intangibles	1,960	1,917
Total assets	**21,623**	**20,834**
Accounts payable & accrued expenses	3,714	3,905
Loans and notes payable	5,112	4,795
Current maturities of long-term debt	261	21
Accrued taxes	769	600
Total current liabilities	9,856	9,321
Long-term debt	854	835
Other long term liabilities	902	1,004
Deferred income taxes	498	358
Total liabilities	12,110	11,518
Common stock	867	870
Capital surplus	2,584	3,196
Reinvested earnings	20,773	21,265
Less treasury stock	(14,711)	(16,015)
Total equity	9,513	9,316
Total liabilities and equity	**21,623**	**20,834**

EXERCISE 42 ▶
Coke's cash flow from ops

Calculate Coca-Cola's 2000 Cash Flow from Operations

Calculate Coca-Cola's cash flow from operations in 2000 using the template below, the income statement and balance sheet on the previous page and the following additional information:

Additional information

- Assume Coca-Cola's depreciation in 2000 was $465
- Assume Coca-Cola's amortization in 2000 was $308
- Assume no sales of intangibles
- Assume there were no other non-cash items on Coca-Cola's income statement in 2000.

Operating current assets and liabilities template

To make sure cash flow statement shorter, add the cashflows from changes in from operating assets and liabilities.

	(Increase)/Decrease
Trade receivables	☐
Inventories	☐
Prepaid expenses	☐
Total (increase)/decrease in operating assets	☐

	Increase/(Decrease)
Accounts payable	☐
Accrued taxes	☐
Deferred taxes	☐
Other long-term liabilities	☐
Total increase/(decrease) in operating liabilities	☐

Simplified operating cash flow template

Net income *(From I/S)*	☐
+ Depreciation of PPE *(From assumptions)*	☐
+ Amortization of intangibles *(From assumptions)*	☐
+ Other non-cash adjustments *(From assumptions)*	☐
(Increase) or decrease in operating assets**	☐
Increase or (decrease) in operating liabilities**	☐
Cash flow from operations	☐

***Use the answer from the template above*

EXERCISE 43 ▶
Coke's cash flow from investments

Calculate Coca-Cola's 2000 Cash Flow from Investing

Calculate Coca-Cola's cash flow from Investing activities in 2000 using the projected income statement and balance sheet, the assumptions and B A S E analysis templates below (to derive CAPEX, accumulated depreciation, and intangibles).

Assumptions

- Coca-Cola sold fixed assets which originally cost $350m for cash of $127m. They did not make a gain or loss on the sale.

Simplified investing cash flow template

Capital expenditures

Fixed asset sales

Sales (purchases) of intangible assets

(Increase) or decrease in all investments

Cash flow from investing activities

	B A S E analysis Intangibles	
B		1999 balance
A		cash flow
S		amortization
E		2000 balance

	B A S E analysis Gross PP&E	
B		1999 balance
A		capital expenditure
S		see assumptions
E		2000 balance

EXERCISE 44 ▶
*Coke's cash flow
from financing*

Calculate Coca-Cola's 2001 Cash Flow from Financing

Calculate Coca-Cola's cash flow from financing activities in 2001 using the projected income statement and balance sheet, the assumptions below, and the B A S E analysis templates in the margin.

Do not include interest payments in your cash flow from financing activities. Interest payments already appeared in net income.

Net increase or (decrease) of short-term debt

Increase (decrease) in long-term debt

(Repurchase of shares (treasury stock))

Equity issuance

(Dividends)

Cash flows from financing activities

B A S E analysis Retained earnings	
B	
A	
S	
E	

Putting the Cash Flow Statement Together

You have calculated the cash flows from:

- **Operational activities**
- **Investing activities**
- **Financing activities**

Now you can put the whole cash flow statement together. When you add up the above three cash flows you get the net cash flow for the year.

How do you know it's right? Check your results against the balance sheet.

Check your results against the balance sheet

How to check your net cash flow results

1. Calculate net change in cash from the balance sheet

	Ending cash	*This year's ending cash balance*
−	Beginning cash	*Last year's ending cash balance*
	Net change in cash	

2. Check net change in cash from the balance sheet against net change in cash from the cash flow statement

Balance sheet		**Cash flow statement**
Net change in cash	***must equal***	Net change in cash

If these two numbers aren't equal, you have made a mistake in your cash flow statement!

EXERCISE 45▶
Coke's projected cash flow

The Cash Flow Statement: Summary

1. Calculate the new cash balance for 2000 using your answers from the previous exercise.

Beginning cash balance
From Coke's 1999 balance sheet

Cash flow from operations

Cash flow from investing activities

Cash flow from financing activities

Ending cash balance

2. Compare your ending cash balance with the cash balance on the 2000 balance sheet. Are they the same?   ❑ Yes   ❑ No

"Cash is king". . .

. . .because it cannot be manipulated

Recap: Why is Cash Flow so Important?

Why do so many managers and experienced financial analysts frequently say that cash is king? Mainly because no one can manipulate cash flows. *(Companies can manipulate their net income figures because GAAP gives them choices about how they can account for transactions. For example, a company can choose between LIFO, FIFO, and the average cost methods when accounting for inventory.)*

Companies who are in financial difficulty pay particular attention to cash flows. If you can't pay your bills on time you risk going into default and out of business even though you might be profitable. Small businesses who have little cash reserves must constantly consider their cash flows.

Lenders are also interested in cash flow because it reflects the ability of a company to repay its debt. In a difficult situation cash flow, not profitability, reflects whether lenders will be repaid or not.

25

EXERCISE 46▶
Go for the gold

Cash Flow Mastery

Use the following balance sheets, income statement and additional information to create a cash flow statement.

Include every balance sheet account except cash! *The check boxes will help you track the accounts you have included on the cash flow statement.*

BALANCE SHEET	2000	2001
Cash and cash equivalents	35,406	39,985
❑ Accounts receivable	12,514	15,450
❑ Inventories	12,616	15,065
❑ Other current assets	7,527	8,000
Total current assets	68,063	78,500
❑ Gross PP&E	100,000	115,000
❑ Accumulated Depreciation	40,400	45,000
Net PP&E	59,600	70,000
❑ Investments	1,000	900
❑ Other non-current assets	2,411	3,000
Total assets	**131,074**	**152,400**
❑ Accounts payable	16,592	18,000
❑ Current portion of long-term debt	448	800
Total current liabilities	17,040	18,800
❑ Long-term debt	31,977	35,000
❑ Other long-term liabilities	3,526	4,500
Total liabilities	52,543	58,300
❑ Common stock	1,000	1,100
❑ APIC	47,761	58,000
❑ Retained earnings	29,770	35,000
Total equity	78,531	94,100
Total liabilities and equity	**131,074**	**152,400**

INCOME STATEMENT	2001
Sales	221,074
COGS excluding depreciation	(178,000)
Depreciation	(5,000)
Gross profit	38,074
SG&A	(23,087)
Operating profit	14,987
Interest expense	(2,679)
Profit before tax	12,308
Taxes	(4,308)
Net income	8,000

continued on next page

B A S E analysis
Accumulated depreciation

Beg

Add

Sub

End

B A S E analysis
Gross PP&E

Beg

Add

Sub

End

B A S E analysis
Retained earnings

Beg

Add

Sub

End

Cash Flow Mastery, continued

Assumptions

- No amortization expense
- Other long-term liabilities are related to operating activities.
- The company sold equipment for $200 cash without a gain or loss. *Hint: Reduction in Gross PP&E = $200 + reduction in Acc. Depn.*

CASH FLOW STATEMENT	2001
Net income	
Depreciation	
(Increase) / decrease in operating assets	
Increase / (decrease) in operating liabilities	
Cash from operations	
Capital expenditures	
Fixed asset sales	
(Increase) / decrease in total investments and other	
Cash from investments	
Increase / (decrease) in long-term debt, including current portion	
Issuance of common stock / APIC	
(Dividends)	
Cash from financing	
Net change in cash	

Check against B/S

B/S beginning cash *(from previous year)*	
B/S ending cash *(from current year)*	
B/S change in cash	

Does net change in cash = B/S change in cash? ❑ Yes ❑ No

Deal #9

_____
your name

_____
value of completed deal

SCORE PAD

1. _____

2. _____

3. _____

4. _____

5. _____

6. _____

7. _____

8. _____

9. _____

10. _____

Total

Close the Deal #9

On to your ninth tombstone! You must make $100,000 to earn this one. If you make less than $100,000, review the material before you go on.

1. Why is the cash flow statement important to financial analysts?

2. What are the three sections of a cash flow statement and what do each of them tell you?

_____

_____

_____

3. Name 3 adjustments you must make to get from net income to cash income.

4. Name three typical investment and three typical financing cash flows:

Investment cash flows	Financing cash flows

continued on next page

Close the Deal #9 continued

5. Assume you sold a building for $10m cash. The building originally cost $8m and you had allocated $5m of depreciation to it. Write out the journal entries you would make to record the sale.

6. If a company's accounts receivable go up, what will happen to cash flow from operations?

   ❏ Go up   ❏ Go down   ❏ Unaffected

7. At the beginning of the year a company had a negative operating working capital of ($4m). During the year operating working capital changed to ($2.5m). Was this change a source or use of cash?

   ❏ Source of cash   ❏ Use of cash

8. A company had other liabilities related to its employee pension plan. Where would changes to this account appear on your cash flow statement?

9. Why are you unlikely to make a published annual report's cash flow statement reconcile to the balance sheet?

10. If a company sells an asset for a loss, is the loss a cash loss or not?

    ❏ cash loss   ❏ non cash loss

Make your
first million

_____

your name

_____

value of completed deal

Score Template

Section 1

Each correct question is worth $20,000. All parts of the question must be correct.

Your score: [   ]

Section 2

Each correct question is worth $25,000. All parts of the question must be correct.

Your score: [   ]

Section 3

Questions 1 – 3: $50,000. All parts of the question must be correct.

Question 4: $450,000

Your score: [   ]

TOTAL SCORE [   ]

Checkout Test for Part 2

Section 1
Understanding the balance sheet and its links with the income statement

1. If Coca-Cola decided to double its inventories, how would the company's balance sheet and cashflow statement be affected? Give your answer in $ and assume that Coke uses short-term debt to meet any funding needs.

[   ]   [   ]

Balance sheet   *Cash flow statement*

2. [   ] Assuming all Coca-Cola's sales are made on credit and its sales figure does not change, what average account receivable balance would the company have had if its receivable days were 35 in 2000?

3. [   ] Assume Coca-Cola adds $400m of patents onto its balance sheet and uses a 40 year period of amortization. What would its amortization expense be each year?

4. What are the benefits and drawbacks of having a large inventory balance? Which is usually preferable, a large or small inventory balance?

[   ]

Benefits of a large inventory balance

[   ]

Drawbacks of a large inventory balance

A ❑ large   ❑ small   inventory balance is usually preferable.

5. a. Which accounts are driven by a company's operations?
   ❑ A deferred tax asset relating to a recent debt issue
   ❑ Accounts receivable net of a bad debt allowance.
   ❑ Short-term debt
   ❑ Prepaid expenses
   ❑ Accrued expenses
   ❑ Accounts payable

   b. If the company increased its balance of accrued expenses, what would be the effect on cashflow from operating activities?
   ❑ Go up   ❑ Go down

6. If all Coca-Cola's competitors had lower receivable days, what would this tell you about Coca-Cola?

7. Name the main link between the income statement and these accounts:

Income statement	Account
Cost of goods sold	Inventories
Example	
	Prepaid insurance on the CEO's car
	Accrued rent on the factory
	Accrued rent on the head office
	Wages payable for the sales force
	Accounts receivable
	Deferred taxes
	Cash
	Debt

8. Which are easier to manipulate, accounts driven by...?
   ❏ Operations   ❏ Financing activities

9. Suppose Coke decides to increase its long-term debt by an additional $500m borrowed at an interest rate of 7.8%. Which accounts on the balance sheet and income statement would be affected, and by how much?

Balance sheet   *Income statement*

10. a. Assume Coca-Cola built an additional bottling plant in Atlanta for $300m. They decided to depreciate the plant over 15 years using their normal method of depreciation *(see the notes)*. How will this affect the company's PP&E accounts *(show only the extra amounts)* and income statement in over the next three years? Assume the plant will have no salvage value.

b. If in 2001 Coca-Cola spent $1,000m on capital expenditure, sold no PP&E and expensed $450m worth of depreciation, what would be its ending 2001 net PP&E?

c. Assume that Coca-Cola decided to sell the bottling plant after one year. The finance department negotiated a sales price of $290m. Write the journal entries for this sale. *(Hint: remember depreciation).*

Section 2 — *Equity accounts, the income statement and taxes*

1. Assume Coca-Cola issued an additional $100m of equity on January 1 2001. It sold each share for $65. Each share had a par value of $0.25. Show the journal entries.

2. If in 2001 Coca-Cola generated $3,200m net income and paid $1,500 of dividends, what would be its 2001 ending reinvested earnings balance?

3. a. Suppose Coca-Cola purchased $500m of its own shares on January 1, 2001. Show the the journal entries for the transaction.

```



```

b. When Coca-Cola purchases treasury stock what happens to the number of its outstanding and issued shares?

Issued shares ☐ Increase ☐ Decrease ☐ Remain the same
Outstanding shares ☐ Increase ☐ Decrease
☐ Remain the same

4. a. Where do you think Coca-Cola adds most of its depreciation to its income statement? ☐ COGS ☐ SG&A

b. Where would it expense amortization?
☐ COGS ☐ SG&A

5. a. What type of costs are cost of goods sold?

```



```

b. Suppose Coca-Cola found a new way to make Coke which dramatically reduced its production costs. What impact would you expect the new process to have on its income statement?

```



```

6. a. Calculate Coca-Cola's average interest expense for 2000. Use the average outstanding debt between 1999 and 2000.

b. A retailing company has a 15% average cost of debt (calculated using the method in 6a. when current interest rates are around 5%). How could you explain this?

```



```

7. a. What are the two tests for extraordinary items?

```



```

```



```

b. Where are extraordinary items normally shown on the income statement?

8. If your tax expense for the year was $100m and you paid the IRS $70m in cash, how would you show the journal entries?

Section 3   *The cash flow statement*

1. If a company has accounts payable of $120m one year and $90m the next year, how much cash was generated or used up during the year?

was ❑ generated   ❑ used up

2. If a company's capital expenditure is equal to its depreciation charge what does this tell you about its fixed asset investment policy?

3. How would your company's cash flow change if:
   a. You increase your receivables from $40m to $80m.

❑ Up   ❑ Down   ❑ No change

   b. You embark on a major investment program increasing capital expenditure from $50m to $150m.

❑ Up   ❑ Down   ❑ No change

   c. Your cost of goods sold as a percentage of sales increases while total sales are static.

❑ Up   ❑ Down   ❑ No change

   d. You decide to start a share buy back program (treasury stock) amounting to $10m a year.

❑ Up   ❑ Down   ❑ No change

4. Use the following information to calculate a cashflow statement:

Income statement for the year to December 31, 2000

All figures in millions	**12/31/00**
Sales	$1,556
Cost of goods sold	(989)
Depreciation	(100)
Gross profit	467
SG&A	(78)
Amortization	(12)
Operating profit	377
Interest expense	(11)
Interest income	5
Profit before tax	371
Taxation	(130)
Net income	241

Balance sheet

	12/31/99	**12/31/00**
Assets		
Cash	50	208
Accounts receivable	180	210
Inventory	120	150
Total current assets	350	568
Gross PP&E	500	610
Depreciation	(350)	(400)
Net PP&E	150	210
Intangibles	245	233
Total assets	**745**	**1,011**
Liabilities		
Accounts payable	100	114
Accrued expenses	45	54
Deferred tax liability	10	12
Current portion of LTD	100	100
Total current liabilities	255	280
Long term debt	300	340
Other liabilities	20	24
Total liabilities	575	644
Common stock	10	12
APIC	20	24
Treasury stock	(5)	(5)
Retained earnings	145	336
Total equity	170	367
Total liabilities & equity	**745**	**1,011**

Additional information
a. Capex was $180m in 1995.
b. You sold equipment for $20m cash (its book value) in 1995.
c. Your deferred tax liability was created by an operating activity.

Cash flow template

Net income	
+ Depreciation of PPE	
+ Amortization	
+/–Other non-cash adjustments	
(Increase) / decrease in operating assets	
Increase / (decrease) in operating liabilities	

Cash from operations

Capital expenditures	
Fixed asset sales	
(Increase) / decrease in other non-operating assets	

Cash from investments

Increase / (decrease) in long-term debt including current portion	
Increase / (decrease) in common stock / APIC	
Increase / (decrease) in other equity accounts	
(Dividends)	

Cash from financing

Net change in cash

Check against B/S

B/S beginning cash *(from previous year)*	
B/S ending cash *(from current year)*	
B/S change in cash	

Does net change in cash = B/S change in cash? ❑ Yes ❑ No

Part Three:
Ratio Analysis

Ratio Analysis
1. Introduction to Ratios

As a financial analyst, you'll spend a great deal of your time comparing companies and analyzing their performance.

Financial statements are useful raw materials for analysis and comparison. However, comparing different companies' numbers directly is misleading, so you will use *ratios*. Ratios help you compare different companies' relative performance even if the companies are very different in size.

The three areas of performance that interest analysts are:

- **Profitability**
- **Capital efficiency**
- **Financial management**

About ratios

Remember that income statements show a summary of an entire time period, while balance sheets are a snapshot of conditions at one moment in time. When you use ratios to determine profitability, follow this general rule:

*Financial
analysis tip*

General ratio rule

When you compare an **income statement** number with a **balance sheet** number, average the balance sheets' current and previous years' figures.

---

2. Profitability

Ratio driver

EXERCISE 1 ▶
Coke's ROE

Profitability is the core of a company's success. A key measure of profitability is the company's **return on equity** (ROE). Return on equity is the percentage of net income divided by average shareholders' equity (*net worth*):

$$\text{ROE} = \frac{\text{Net income}}{(\text{this year's net worth} + \text{last year's net worth}) * \frac{1}{2}}$$

Note: Net worth = total shareholders' equity

If net income **rises** and net worth **remains the same:**　　ROE rises
If net income **stays the same** and net worth **falls:**　　ROE rises

If net income **falls** and net worth **remains the same:**　　ROE falls
If net income **stays the same** and net worth **rises:**　　ROE falls

Return on Equity

1. Calculate Coca-Cola's ROE for the last three years.

1998	1999	2000

2. What drives the ROE number. . .

. . .on the income statement?

. . .on the balance sheet?

3. Compare Coca-Cola's ROE for 2000 *(Question 1)* with its major competitor PepsiCo Inc.'s ROE over the last three years:

	1998	1999	2000
Pepsi	30%	31%	31%

Which company is more profitable?　❑ Coca-Cola　❑ PepsiCo

4. Do the same analysis with gross margin for Coca-Cola over the last three years and compare it with PepsiCo Inc:

	1998	1999	2000
Coke			
Pepsi	58.3%	59.7%	61.1%

Which company has a higher gross margin?
❑ Coca-Cola　❑ PepsiCo

5. How could Coca-Cola increase its ROE?
❑ By increasing dividends　❑ By reducing dividends

Ratio driver

Too few assets?

Return on equity

Companies can increase profitability (ROE) three ways:

- **Generate a higher proportion of net income for each $1 of sales**
- **Reduce the amount of assets needed to support a given amount of sales**
- **Reduce the proportion of assets funded by equity**

$$ROE = \frac{Net\ income}{Sales} \times \frac{Sales}{Average\ assets} \times \frac{Average\ assets}{Average\ equity}$$

Companies can have too few assets. If a company has too few assets per $1 of sales it might have trouble responding quickly to customers' needs.

Example   If inventory is too low, sudden demand could clean out the company's shelves, leaving customers frustrated.

EXERCISE 2 ▶
Coke's vs. Pepsi's ROE

Comparing Two Companies' ROE's

1. Calculate the components of Coca-Cola's return on equity in 2000:

$\dfrac{Net\ Income}{Sales}$ $\dfrac{Sales}{Avg.\ assets}$ $\dfrac{Avg.\ assets}{Avg.\ total\ equity}$

2. Compare them to PepsiCo Inc's numbers:
   PepsiCo   ROE(2000) = 31%   10.7% * 1.139 * 2.540

   What drives the difference between Coke's and Pepsi's ROE?

3. If you were the CEO of Coke, what would you do?

3. Capital Efficiency

It's easy to assume that the more assets a company has the better. However, as a financial analyst you are only interested in the asset value of the business *if you are going to break it up and sell it.* Otherwise you are more interested in the cash and ultimately the dividends the company can generate over time for its stockholders.

Funding costs money

Assets need to be funded and funding with debt and equity costs money.

Financial analysis tip

- **If your company takes out a loan, it must pay interest. If it doesn't, the bank can sue.**
- **If you raise money from investors in the form of equity, they expect you to pay them dividends, although they can't force you to do so. If you want to raise equity in the future and increase the price of your equity in the market, you will make sure your returns to your investors are as high as possible.**

More assets require more funding, which means. . .

  . . .More **debt,** which means. . .

    . . .Higher interest expense, which means. . .

      . . .Lower net income, which means. . .

        . . .Lower ROE

              OR

More funding means. . .

  . . .More **equity,** which means. . .

    . . .Lower ROE.

Shareholder value

You'll hear this a lot on the Street

Wall Street measures shareholder value through the stock market and a company's share price. You'll hear financial analysts talk about maximizing shareholder value. A company increases shareholder value by increasing returns to its shareholders.

EXERCISE 3 ▶
Coke's shareholder value

Shareholder Value

1. [box] How much money did Coca-Cola pay to its debt holders in 2000?

2. [box] What dividends did Coca-Cola pay to its equity holders in 2000?

3. If you increase shareholder value, will your stock price
   ❑ Fall   ❑ Rise   ❑ Remain unchanged

Current assets and shareholder value

You've already seen how reducing assets can increase a company's profitability. A critical day-to-day responsibility of management is keeping current assets as low as possible without affecting customer service.

Low assets per $ of sales means. . .

. . .Higher profitability, which means. . .

. . .Higher share price, which means. . .

. . .Greater shareholder value.

EXERCISE 4 ▶
CA levels and profitability

Current Asset Levels

1. Calculate Coca-Cola's inventory days and receivable days for 2000. Use the average balance of inventories and receivables.

   [box]   [box]

   Inventory days   **Receivable days**

2. a. [box] If Coca-Cola averaged receivables days of 42, (*if management chased people who owed them money more slowly*), what would their new average receivables be in 2000?

   b. [box] How much more funding would Coca-Cola need ? (*use average numbers*)

   c. [box] If Coca-Cola financed the funding with debt costing 7% per year, how much more interest would they have to pay?

   d. Would shareholders benefit from this move?   ❑ Yes   ❑ No

3. [box] Using the same assumptions as in Question 2, find the extra cost to Coca-Cola if its inventories spent on average ten days longer in the warehouse.

continued on next page

EXERCISE 4 ▶
CA levels and profitability, continued

Financial analysis tip

EXERCISE 5 ▶
Testing information out of CAPEX

Current Asset Levels continued

4. Using the following information calculate PepsiCo's inventory and receivable days:

	1999	2000
Inventories	899	905
Receivables	1,704	1,799
COGS		7,943
Sales		20,438

Inventory days	Receivable days

Long-term assets

The company uses long-term assets to help manufacture its products and house its head office and sales staff. To stay competitive you must continually invest in fixed assets. If you don't, you may find yourself left behind by other companies in the same sector.

If a company's depreciation charge is higher than its capital expenditure, you know the company is using up its fixed assets faster than it is replacing them. In the short term a company can probably get away with this practice. In the long term its competitive position will be eroded.

Hidden Meanings in Capital Expenditure

1. Compare Coca-Cola's depreciation charge to its capital expenditure over the last three years. Is Coca-Cola increasing its fixed assets? *Hint: Find depreciation in Selected Financial Data and CAPEX in the Cash Flow Statement as "Purchases of PP&E."*

   ❏ Yes ❏ No

2. [____] How much net fixed assets did Coca-Cola have in 2000 to support each $1 of sales? *Divide 2000 Net PP&E by 2000 sales.*

3. [____] Use the numbers below to calculate how much net fixed assets PepsiCo needs to support $1 of sales.

PepsiCo	2000
Sales	20,438
Net PP&E	5,438

Current liabilities and shareholder value

Now jump across to the liability side of the balance sheet. Accounts payable is a big number for Coca-Cola. Normally companies will try to increase their payables number as this is "free funding." However, you must be careful not to annoy your suppliers by paying them too late or they might decide not deal with you.

More payables means. . .

. . .More free funding, which means. . .

. . .Greater returns to shareholders, which means. . .

. . .Higher shareholder value

Beware of *too much* free funding

EXERCISE 6 ▶
The payoff in days payable

Days Payable and Shareholder Value

$$\text{Days payable} = \frac{\text{Avg. accounts payable}}{\text{COGS}} \times 365$$

1. [   ] What was Coca-Cola's days payable in 2000? *(Use the accounts payable and accrued expenses figure in note 4.)*

2. Does Coca-Cola have to pay interest on its accounts payable?
   ❑ Yes ❑ No

3. Use your answer to Question 1 and the information below to compare Coca-Cola's and PepsiCo's average days payable to sales.

PepsiCo	1999	2000
Accs. payable & accruals	3,399	3,815
COGS		7,943

Which company has a higher days payable?
❑ Coca-Cola ❑ PepsiCo

4. Financial Management

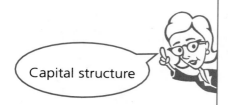

Capital structure

Debt and shareholder value

The owners of debt have first claim on the assets of a company. They can also demand the interest payments due to them. In return for these benefits, they accept a lower return on their investment than owners of equity. The benefit for the company is that debt is cheaper funding than equity.

Companies can increase their profitability by adjusting their **capital structure** (*proportion of debt to equity on the balance sheet*) to provide a higher proportion of debt funding.

Terms you should know

Net debt	=	Total debt – cash
Total capital	=	Net debt + equity

EXERCISE 7 ▶

What does cost of debt do to ROE?

Cost of Debt and ROE

1. [ ]   Calculate Coca-Cola's average cost of debt for 2000. Include all debt and use the average balance between 1999 and 2000.

2. [ ]   What was its return on equity in 2000?

3. [ ]   What was the total capital (total net debt plus total shareholders' equity) that Coca-Cola "employed" (this is the financial term) in 2000

4. Calculate Coca-Cola's net income in 2000 if the company had replaced $2b of its equity with debt. Use your average cost of debt for Coca-Cola in 2000 (*from Question 1*) and assume a tax rate of 31%.

[ ]	Step 1.	Find the increase in interest expense.
[ ]	Step 2.	What was Coca-Cola's original income before tax in 2000?

continued on next page

EXERCISE 7 ▶

What does cost of debt do to ROE?, continued

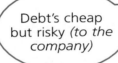

Cost of Debt and ROE, continued

	Step 3.	Subtract the increase in interest expense from income before tax.
	Step 4.	Calculate net income using a 31% tax rate.
	Step 5.	Recalculate Coca-Cola's ROE using your new net income and total stockholders' equity figures. *(Assume retained earnings does not change.)*

5. You have swapped equity for debt. What happened to Coke's ROE?

   ❏ Went up   ❏ Went down

Debt's cheap but risky *(to the company)*

Consequences of debt funding

Why don't companies raise funds just from debt? Because a higher level of debt has consequences:

Consequence 1:   The company's interest cost (as a % of debt raised) rises *(**leverage** costs)*.

Consequence 2:   The company is more vulnerable in downturns *(measured by interest **coverage**)*.

Leverage

A high proportion of debt scares a company's debt holders. They are concerned that if the company goes bust, they may not get all their money back.

When a company fails, the assets are sold for cash. The cash is then returned, first to the debt holders, then to the equity holders. But sometimes the cash received from the assets is not enough to pay everyone back. The larger the debt, the more likely that the debt holders could be in the group that loses out and doesn't get paid back.

Analysts use leverage to measure this risk. The proportion of debt to equity capital is called a company's ***leverage ratio.*** The higher a company's leverage, the higher a company's cost of debt, as the debt holders' risk increases.

$$\text{Leverage ratio} = \frac{\text{Net debt}}{\text{Total equity}}$$

Financial analysis tip

EXERCISE 8 ▶
Bankruptcy risk

> GULP!
> *have* to pay that
> interest . . .

Leverage ratio

1. Calculate Coca-Cola's leverage ratio for the last two years.

	1999	2000
Coke's leverage ratio	☐	☐

2. Compare your answer to question 1 with PepsiCo's leverage ratio for the last two years:

	1999	2000
Net debt / total equity	30%	21%

Which company has a riskier debt-to-equity ratio?
☐ Coke   ☐ PepsiCo

Interest and risk assessment

Another aspect of risk that concerns debt holders is a company's ability to pay interest. The greater proportion of debt a company has, the more pretax income it will have to use to pay interest to its debt holders.

Interest payments are compulsory. A company can't "choose" to pay them like dividend payments. Therefore if a company's earnings take a downturn, its interest payments may eat up all the company's net income, and then some.

One way to measure a company's ability to meet its interest payments and still make a profit is to calculate *interest coverage* (how many times its interest payment is "covered" by earnings available to pay interest).

One ratio you can use to calculate coverage is *times interest earned.*

$$\text{Times interest earned} = \frac{\text{Earnings before int. exp and tax (EBIT)**}}{\text{Interest expense}}$$

**Note: Excludes interest income*

Companies with stable earnings, like utility companies, can support a low *times interest earned* ratio. They can be relatively certain that their earnings won't fluctuate and they can manage to pay interest without losses in nearly all years. Companies with unstable earnings such as airlines can't profitably carry such high levels of debt.

EXERCISE 9 ▶
Times interest earned

Deal #10

_____
your name

_____
value of completed deal

SCORE PAD

1. _____

2. _____

3. _____

4. _____

5. _____

6. _____

7. _____

8. _____

9. _____

10. _____

Total

Times Interest Earned

1. Calculate Coca-Cola's ltimes interest earned for the last three years.

	1998	1999	2000
Times interest earned			

2. Compare your answer to question 1 with Pepsi's times interest earned:

	1998	1999	2000
Times interest earned	6.7x	11.1x	15.5x

Which company's debt holders face more risk in 2000?
❑ Coca-Cola   ❑ PepsiCo

Close the Deal #10

It's time for you to earn your last tombstone! You must make $100,000 to earn this tombstone. If you make less than $100,000, review the material before you go on.

1. Name three ways a company can increase its profitability:
   Hint: Think about the components of ROE

2. Examine the following companies. Which one has the highest ROE?

	$\dfrac{\text{Net income}}{\text{Sales}}$	$\dfrac{\text{Sales}}{\text{Average assets}}$	$\dfrac{\text{Average assets}}{\text{Average total equity}}$
❑ A.	25.0%	0.20	2.00
❑ B.	10.0%	1.54	3.25
❑ C.	5.0%	2.00	3.25

3. At the beginning of the year a company's average days payable is 60 days. During the year its average days payable falls to 40 days. How does this change affect the company's financing needs and income statement? Assume any new funding it requires will be met by additional debt.

   Debt funding   ❑ rises   ❑ falls
   Net income   ❑ rises   ❑ falls

4. Companies can increase their profitability if they increase their leverage. Then why don't all companies fund themselves with 100% debt?

continued on next page

Close the Deal #10 continued

5. What are the positive and negative impacts of having high levels of current assets?

Positive

Negative

6. Consider the following capital expenditure and depreciation schedule for a large manufacturing company:

	1996	1997	1998	1999	2000
Capex	100	120	150	130	145
Depn.	150	140	120	120	125

What is the net increase / (decrease) in net PP&E between 1991 and 1995? Assume there are no sales and retirements.

7. If a company increases its proportion of debt to equity, how will this decision affect the following?

ROE	❑ rises	❑ falls
Net income	❑ rises	❑ falls

8. A company's net earnings before interest expense and tax are $2,000. Its interest expense is $500. What is its times interest earned?

9. Two firms have the following leverage ratios. Which is riskier to debt holders?

Leverage	1999	2000
❑ Company A	150%	140%
❑ Company B	20%	40%

10. Two firms have the following times interest earned ratios. Which is riskier to debt holders?

Times interest earned	1999	2000
❑ Company A	4.5	5.0
❑ Company B	0.9	1.0

The End – Almost

That's it! You have covered the essential aspects of accounting that you need to know for financial analysis. The last task you have to do is complete your last deal – it's for a billion dollars – and check your score.

Your Billion Dollar Deal

Billion $ Deal

_____
your name

_____
value of completed deal

Your last deal is the big one: it's worth $1,000,000,000.

If you are not clear about any of the subjects you've covered, review them now.

Good luck!

Instructions

You will need:
❏ Pen or pencil
❏ Paper
❏ Calculator
❏ Your copy of Coca-Cola's 2000 annual report

The final bonus exam is split into two parts:
❏ Basic accounting
❏ Understanding the financial statements

Answers are in the answer booklet.

Turn the page to begin

1. Basic Accounting

1. Look at Coca-Cola's equity accounts for 2000. Use the assumptions below to forecast the company's equity accounts for 2001. Then calculate the return on equity for 2001.

- **$200m of new equity was issued for $58 per share with a par value of $0.25.**
- **Accumulated comprehensive income stayed constant throughout the year.**
- **Assume Coca-Cola generated $2,300 of net income in 2001.**
- **Assume that Coca-Cola purchased 9,500,000 of its own shares at $59 each during the year.**
- **Assume that Coca-Cola declared and paid dividends amounting to $1,125m during 2001.**

Equity accounts, 2001

Account	Amount
Common stock	
Capital surplus	
Reinvested earnings	
Accumulated other comprehensive income and unearned compensation	
Treasury stock	
Total equity	

Return on equity, 2001

2. a. [   ] Using the following assumptions for Coca-Cola's current asset and liability accounts in 2001, calculate Coke's new working capital balance.

- **In 2001 Coca-Cola's inventory, trade receivables and accounts payable remain the same percent of sales as in 2000.**
- **In 2001 Coca-Cola increases its sales by $3,545m.**
- **Cash and marketable securities remain the same percent of sales as in 2000.**
- **Accrued taxes are 7.55% of sales.**
- **Prepaid expenses and other assets increase by $537m in 2001.**

- ■ Coke increases its short-term debt financing by $139m in 2001.
- ■ Find current maturities of long-term debt in the notes.

b. If a company has a higher receivables-to-sales ratio than its main competitors, what does this suggest?

3. Assume that Coca-Cola began a major capital expenditure program in 2001, outlined below. Assume all new assets are depreciated over four years and have a salvage value of 15% of their original cost.

Determine the additions to Coca-Cola's PP&E accounts.

$ millions	2001	2002	2003
New CAPEX at beg. of year	950	1,000	1,050

Additions to Gross PP&E:

Additions to Accumulated Depreciation

4. a. Assume Coca-Cola improved its gross margin by 1.5% in 2001. Name two possible reasons for the improvement.

b. If Coca-Cola's depreciation expense was $298m instead of $465m in 2000, how would the following numbers change, if at all?

I/S   Operating income (operating profit)

B/S   Net PP&E

CFS   Net cash flow (assume no tax effect)

c. Suppose Coca-Cola decided to use its $1,819m of cash and cash equivalents and its $73m worth of current marketable securities to pay off first its short-term debt and then its long-term debt balances. What would happen to:

Total assets?	❑ Rise	❑ Fall	❑ Remain the same
Interest income?	❑ Rise	❑ Fall	❑ Remain the same
Interest expense?	❑ Rise	❑ Fall	❑ Remain the same
Leverage ratio?	❑ Rise	❑ Fall	❑ Remain the same

4. d. Assume Coca-Cola uses straight-line depreciation for its GAAP financial statements that it shows to its shareholders and accelerated depreciation for calculating taxes due to the government. If Coca-Cola undertook a large CAPEX program, would its net income be higher under its GAAP financial statements or its tax accounts next year?

❑ GAAP   ❑ Tax

5. Using some of the information below, calculate SoupCo's cash provided by operating activities in 2000:

- **SoupCo reduced its account receivable balance by $33m in 2000.**
- **Amortization was $29m in 2000.**
- **Long-term deferred income taxes (liability) increased by $59m in 2000.**
- **Capital expenditure was $441m in 2000.**
- **During the year SoupCo repaid $41m of long-term borrowings.**
- **Depreciation expense was $332m in 2000.**
- **Inventories increased by $45m in 2000.**
- **During the year SoupCo repurchased $19m of treasury stock.**
- **In 1995 SoupCo's other current assets increased by $41m. Its other current liabilities fell by $14m. Both accounts were driven by operating decisions.**
- **Other long-term liabilities related to employee pension obligations increased by $15m during the same year.**
- **Net income was $632m in 2000.**

┌─────────────────────────┐
│   │ Cash provided by operations
└─────────────────────────┘

2. Financial Statements

1. Use the following information to project Coca-Cola's income statement and balance sheet through 2001.

Show your answers in millions.

Income statement assumptions for 2001

- During the year Coca-Cola generated $25,000m of sales.
- Coca-Cola's SG&A expense was $9,452m *(includes amortization)*.
- There was no other income, equity income or gain on issuance of stock.
- Coca-Cola's COGS was $10,807m *(includes depreciation)*.
- Assume interest income was $250m and interest expense was $280m.
- Coca-Cola's effective tax rate was 31% in 2001.
- Other operating charges remained the same.

Balance sheet assumptions for 2001

- Coca-Cola paid $1,500m of dividends.
- On December 31 2001 Coca-Cola had increased its inventory balance by $381m and its trade accounts receivable by $405m.
- Coca-Cola's current marketable securities increased by $22m during the year and its long-term marketable securities and other assets increased by $19m.
- Coca-Cola's accounts payable and accrued expenses increased by $1,606m in 2001.
- Coca-Cola spent $1,200m on capital expenditure during 2001 and its depreciation expense was $597m. Coca-Cola sold PP&E for $140m cash. It originally cost $540m and had $400m of accumulated depreciation allocated to it.
- During the year assume Coca-Cola purchased no other companies or patents and its amortization expense was $50m.
- Coca-Cola issued an additional $400m of long-term debt. *Remember you can find the repayment schedule of Coca-Cola's existing long-term debt in the notes.*
- Coca-Cola bought $897m of its own stock during the year for $62 per share.
- Accrued taxes increased by $73m and deferred taxes increased by $11m.
- Coca-Cola issued no new shares during the year.
- Other liabilities related to employee pensions fell by $(124)m.
- There was no change to unearned compensation related to outstanding restricted stock.
- Prepaid expenses and other assets increased by $89m in 1996.
- There was no change to equity method or cost method investments.

- Cash and equivalents grew to $2,660m.
- Assume Coca-Cola issued notes payable to make up any funding shorfall.

Coca-Cola
Projected income statement, 2001

Coca-Cola Projected income statement	2000	2001 (Proj.)
	Assets	

Coca-Cola		2001
Projected balance sheet	2000	(Projected)
Liabilities & Equity		

2. Calculate a cashflow statement for 2001 using the format you learned in Part 2. Check your answer against the change in cash from your balance sheet. Check off each balance sheet account to make sure you have included them all.

Coca-Cola
Cash flow statement, 2001

3. a. Calculate the constituents of ROE for Coca-Cola in 2001. How has it changed from 2000? Explain why the numbers have changed.

$\dfrac{\text{Net income}}{\text{Sales}}$	$\times$	$\dfrac{\text{Sales}}{\text{Average assets}}$	$\times$	$\dfrac{\text{Average assets}}{\text{Average equity}}$

2001 ROE

Why ROE changed

b. Calculate Coca-Cola's gross and operating margins in 2001.

Gross margin   *Operating margin*

c. Calculate Coca-Cola's working capital in 2000 and 2001.

Working capital, 2000   *Working capital, 2001*

4. Calculate the following ratios for Coca-Cola in 2001:

Depreciation / capital expenditure

Accum depn / Gross PP&E

5. a. Calculate Coca-Cola's leverage ratio in 2000 and 2001. Why has it changed?

Leverage ratio, 2000   *Leverage ratio, 2001*

Why the numbers changed

b. Calculate Coca-Cola's times interest earned in 2000 and 2001. Why has it changed?

Times interest earned, 2000

Times interest earned, 2001

Why the ratio changed

END OF BILLION DOLLAR DEAL

Appendix 1: Debits and Credits

Try these drills if you are having trouble with debits and credits. The best way to grasp debits and credits is through practice. The concept isn't hard; it just doesn't make sense at first.

Just keep doing the exercises and the concept will sink in.

DRILL 1 ▶
Debits and credits

Debits and Credits

Below is a list of increases and decreases in balance sheet accounts. Would the entry be a debit or credit?

1. You increase your cash balance by $10,000.
   ❑ Debit   ❑ Credit

2. You reduce your long term debt by $30,000.
   ❑ Debit   ❑ Credit

3. You increase your paid-in-capital by $5,000.
   ❑ Debit   ❑ Credit

4. You pay dividends of $1,000.
   ❑ Debit   ❑ Credit

5. You increase inventories by $500.
   ❑ Debit   ❑ Credit

6. You decrease inventories by $2,000.
   ❑ Debit   ❑ Credit

7. You increase accounts receivable by $8,000.
   ❑ Debit   ❑ Credit

8. You decrease cash by $300.
   ❑ Debit   ❑ Credit

9. You pay back $2,000 of short term debt.
   ❑ Debit   ❑ Credit

10. You purchase a car for $10,000.
    ❑ Debit   ❑ Credit

DRILL 2 ▶
Low-cost housing

Low-Cost Housing in New York

Assume you invest in a new building company providing low-cost housing in New York City. You volunteered to help with the book-keeping for the company.

Part 1
Complete the journal entries. You'll use them to build your balance sheet.

1. You and four friends each invest $200,000 in the new company in return for shares.

2. A plot of development land comes up for sale. The company purchases it using $100,000 of cash and a 5-year loan of $300,000.

3. The company purchases a small digging machine for $50,000. The manufacturer gives free credit for 90 days (accounts payable). You expect the machine to last at least 3 years.

4. The company makes the following purchases of building materials (inventory).
   - $40,000 worth of bricks, paying in cash
   - $35,000 worth of cement. The supplier gives 90 days credit.
   - $7,000 worth of glass. You pay in cash.

5. Two more sites come up for sale. One costs $200,000, the other $300,000. The first site is paid for in cash. The second is paid for using $150,000 of cash and a new $150,000 long-term loan.

continued on next page

DRILL 2 ▶

Low-cost housing, continued

Low Cost Housing in New York, continued

Part 2
First make sure your debits equal your credits, then use your journal entries to help create a balance sheet for the company after the five transactions shown in part 1.

1. [   ]   [   ]

     Total debits   **=**   Total credits

Correct any problems so that total debits = total credits.

2. Create a balance sheet for the company based on the information in part 1.

Balance sheet

Assets		Liabilities	
Cash	[ ]		[ ]
	[ ]	**Total CL**	[ ]
Total CA	[ ]		
	[ ]		[ ]
Tot. NCA	[ ]	**Tot. Liabs.**	[ ]
			[ ]
		Tot. Eq.	[ ]
Tot. Assets	[ ]	**Tot. L&E**	[ ]

DRILL 3 ▶
More debits and credits

Debits and Credits and the Income Statement

Write out the journal entries for each transaction.

1. You purchased a new car for $30,000 paying in cash.

2. You make $100,000 worth of sales, all paid for in cash.

3. The goods you sold cost $80,000 to manufacture.

4. You paid your accountant a $1,000 fee in cash.

5. The bank charged you interest of $1,000. You paid in cash.

6. You purchased inventory worth $5,000. The supplier gave you credit.

7. You take out a long term loan for $50,000. The bank gives you cash.

continued on next page

DRILL 3 ▶
More debits and credits continued

Debits and Credits and the Income Statement, continued

8. During the year you pay **$8,000** worth of dividends in cash.

9. The Internal Revenue Service charges you **$8,500** in tax. You pay them in cash.

10. You make a further **$30,000** in sales. This time you give all your customers credit.

DRILL 4 ▶
Building a balance sheet and income statement using debits and credits

Building a Balance Sheet and Income Statement

First write out the journal entries for the transactions below. You'll use them to create a balance sheet and income statement.

1. You invest **$1,000,000** of cash to set up your new computer retailing business. You record your investment as paid-in capital on the balance sheet.

2. You purchase a warehouse for **$500,000**, paying cash.

3. You take out a long-term loan from your bank for **$2,000,000**. The bank gives you cash.

continued on next page

Building a Balance Sheet and Income Statement, continued

4. You purchase $1,750,000 worth of inventory (computers) during the year. You are given credit for $500,000 of the purchase. You pay the remainder in cash.

5. During the year you make $2,500,000 worth of sales. Half of these sales were for cash and half on credit.

6. You employed 2 administrative staff and 2 salespeople. Their salaries totalled $200,000 during the year. Record this as an SG&A expense. You pay all salaries with cash.

7. The bank charged you $200,000 worth of interest. You paid them in cash.

8. The sales you made during the year cost you $1,500,000 to generate.

9. The government charged you $200,000 in taxes during the year. You paid them in cash.

10. You purchased a car for $30,000 paying in cash.

continued on next page

DRILL 4 ▶

Building a balance sheet and income statement using debits and credits, continued

Building a Balance Sheet and Income Statement, continued

INCOME STATEMENT

Revenue/sales

Cost of goods sold

Gross profit

SG&A

Operating profit

Interest expense

Profit before tax

Tax

Net income

BALANCE SHEET

ASSETS	$000s	LIABILITIES	$000s
Total current assets		**Total current liabilities**	
Total NCA		**Total NCL**	
		TOTAL LIABILITIES	
		TOTAL EQUITY	
TOTAL ASSETS		**TOTAL L&E**	

DRILL 5 ▶
Advanced debits and credits

Using Debits and Credits to Organize Your Work

Assume you recently purchased a greeting card company called Franky C. Cards Inc.. First write our the debits and credits on the table provided. Then recalculate the balance sheet and prepare an income statement. Assume all figures are in millions.

Franky C. Cards Balance Sheet at purchase

ASSETS	$000s	LIABILITIES	$000s
Cash	100	A/C Payable	670
A/C receivable	700	Accrued exp.	60
Inventories	550	Short-term debt	500
Prepaid expenses	50	**Total current liabs.**	**1,230**
Total current assets	**1,400**		
		Long-term debt	700
Net PP&E	960	Other liabilities	89
Investments	570	**Total liabilities**	**2,019**
		Paid-in capital	480
		Retained earnings	431
		Total equity	**911**
Total assets	**2,930**	**Total liabs. & equity**	**2,930**

1. During the year Franky C Cards generated $1,500 of sales during the year. 30% of these sales were on credit and 70% were for cash.

2. The cards sold cost $700 to manufacture.

3. Franky C Cards added $650 to its inventory. The supplier gave Franky C $325 of credit, the remainder was paid in cash.

4. Investments increased by $100, paid for in cash.

5. Franky C's existing investments generated $57 of interest income, paid in cash.

6. Franky C instructed their advertising agency to start an advertising campaign. So far the agency has spent $70. Franky C has accrued this expense on their balance sheet. (Hint: increase SG&A and accrued expenses).

7. The company raised an additional $500 of long term debt. It received cash from the bank.

8. Franky C reduced its short-term debt by $100.

9. They company paid $309 in taxes in cash.

10. Other SG&A expenses amounted to $50 paid in cash.

11. Franky C paid interest of $120 in cash to the bank.

12. Assume no dividends were paid and there was no depreciation recorded.

13. Assume all other accounts remained the same.

continued on next page

DRILL 5 ▶
Advanced debits and credits, continued

Using Debits and Credits to Organize your Work, continued

1. Dr _____ _____
   Dr _____ _____
   Cr _____   _____

2. Dr _____ _____
   Cr _____   _____

3. Dr _____ _____
   Dr _____   _____
   Cr _____   _____

4. Dr _____ _____
   Cr _____   _____

5. Dr _____ _____
   Cr _____   _____

6. Dr _____ _____
   Cr _____   _____

7. Dr _____ _____
   Cr _____   _____

8. Dr _____ _____
   Cr _____   _____

9. Dr _____ _____
   Cr _____   _____

10. Dr _____ _____
    Cr _____   _____

11. Dr _____ _____
    Cr _____   _____

continued on next page

DRILL 5 ▶

*Advanced debits
and credits, continued*

Using Debits and Credits to Organize your Work, continued

INCOME STATEMENT

Revenue/sales
Cost of goods sold
Gross profit

SG&A
Operating profit
Interest income
Interest expense
Profit before tax
Tax
Net income

BALANCE SHEET

ASSETS	$000s	LIABILITIES	$000s
Cash		A/C Payable	
A/C receivable		Accrued exp.	
Inventories		Short term debt	
Prepaid expenses			
Total current assets		**Total current liabilities**	
Net PP&E		Long term debt	
Investments		Other liabilities	
		Total liabilities	
		Paid in capital	
		Retained earnings	
		Total equity	
Total assets		**Total liabilities & equity**	

Appendix 2:
The Cash Flow Statement

If you need more practice with cash flow statements, try this additional cash flow exercise.

DRILL 1 ▶
Colin's diving business

Colin's Cash Flow Statement

Colin recently established a diving business in Key West. Using his balance sheet and income statement below calculate his cash flow statement. Use the BASE tables to help you. Assume the following:

- Colin spent $20 on new equipment.
- There were no sales of fixed assets or intangibles.
- There were no purchases of intangibles.

All figures in thousands.

	INCOME STATEMENT
	2001
Sales	110
COGS	(55)
Depreciation	(5)
Gross profit	50
SG&A	(15)
Amortization	(2)
Operating profit	33
Interest income	2
Interest expense	(5)
Profit before tax	30
Tax	(10)
Net income	20
Dividends	5

continued on next page

DRILL 1 ▶
Colin's diving business, continued

Colin's Cash Flow Statement, continued

Balance sheet	2000	2001
Assets		
Cash	5	10
Trade accounts receivable	50	55
Inventories	35	40
Prepaid expenses	10	12
Total current assets	100	117
Gross PP&E	100	120
Accumulated Depreciation	(50)	(55)
Net PP&E	50	65
Intangibles	10	8
Total assets	**160**	**190**
Liabilities		
Accounts payable & accrued expenses	35	40
Loans and notes payable	10	15
Total current liabilities	45	55
Long term debt	25	30
Total liabilities	70	85
Equity		
Common stock	5	5
Additional paid in capital	45	45
Reinvested earnings	40	55
Total equity	90	105
Total liabilities and equity	**160**	**190**

continued on next page

DRILL 1 ▶
Colin's diving business, continued

Gross PP&E

Beg

Add

Sub

End

Accumulated Depreciation

Beg

Add

Sub

End

Net Intangibles

Beg

Add

Sub

End

Colin's Cash Flow Statement, continued

Now build Colin's cash flow statement, using the available information.

Cash flow statement	2001
Net income	
Depreciation	
Amortization	
(Increase) decrease in operating assets	
Increase (decrease) in operating liabilities	
Cash from operating activities	
Capital expenditure	
Sales of fixed assets	
(Purchase) sale of Intangibles	
Cash from investing activities	
Increase (decrease) in debt	
Increase (decrease) in cmn. stock & APIC	
Dividends	
Cash from financing activities	
Net cash flow	
Beginning cash balance from B/S	
Ending cash balance from B/S	
Difference	

Does Net cash flow = Difference? It should.

DRILL 2 ▶
Patricia's nail salons

Patricia Reed's Cash Flow Statement

Patricia Reed set up a chain of nail salons. Using her balance sheet and income statement, calculate her cash flow statement for 2001. Assume:

■ Patricia has no intangible assets.

■ There were no sales of fixed assets during the year.

■ Other long-term liabilities were related to the company's operating activities

All figures in thousands

Income statement	2000	2001
Sales		1,200
COGS		(900)
Depreciation		(45)
Gross profit		255
SG&A		(89)
Operating profit		166
Interest income		10
Interest expense		(25)
Profit before tax		151
Tax		(47)
Net income		104
Dividends		25

Balance sheet		
Assets		
Cash	47	86
Trade accounts receivable	360	400
Inventories	150	152
Prepaid expenses	15	12
Total current assets	572	650
Investments	74	95
Gross PP&E	213	265
Accumulated Depreciation	(123)	(168)
Net PP&E	90	97
Total assets	736	842
Liabilities		
Accounts payable & accrued expenses	210	215
Loans and notes payable	50	56
Total current liabilities	260	271
Long term debt	251	269
Other long-term liabilities	10	8
Total liabilities	521	548
Equity		
Common stock	5	5
Additional paid-in capital	60	60
Reinvested earnings	150	229
Total equity	215	294
Total liabilities and equity	736	842

DRILL 2 ▶

Patricia's nail salons, continued

Gross PP&E

Beg

Add

Sub

End

Accumulated Depr.

Beg

Add

Sub

End

Patricia's Cash Flow Statement, continued

Cash flow statement	2001
Net income	
Depreciation	
(Increase) decrease in operating assets	
Increase (decrease) in operating liabilities	
Cash from operating activities	
Capital expenditure	
Sales of fixed assets	
(Increase) decrease in other assets	
Cash from investing activities	
Increase (decrease) in debt	
Increase (decrease) in common stock & APIC	
Dividends	
Cash from financing activities	
Net cash flow	
Beginning cash balance from B/S	
Ending cash balance from B/S	
Difference	

Does Net cash flow = Difference? It should.

DRILL 3

Julies boutiques

Julie's boutiques

Julie Curtis established a chain of women's clothing boutiques across New York State. Using her balance sheet and income statement below calculate her cash flow statement. Assume:

- There were no sales of fixed assets during the year.
- Julie has no intangible assets.

All figures in thousands

Income statement	2000	2001
Sales		12,500
COGS		(9,000)
Depreciation		(300)
Gross profit		3,200
SG&A		(2,000)
Operating profit		1,200
Interest income		10
Interest expense		(350)
Profit before tax		860
Tax		(301)
Net income		559
Dividends		140

Balance sheet	2000	2001
Assets		
Cash	800	919
Trade accounts receivable	3,750	4,000
Inventories	3,000	3,500
Prepaid expenses	100	150
Total current assets	7,650	8,569
Investments	100	100
Gross PP&E	5,000	5,500
Accumulated Depreciation	(4,000)	(4,300)
Net PP&E	1,000	1,200
Total assets	8,750	9,869
Liabilities		
Accounts payable	700	800
Loans and notes payable	3,000	3,100
Total current liabilities	3,700	3,900
Long term debt	3,000	3,500
Total liabilities	6,700	7,400
Equity		
Common stock	50	50
Additional paid-in capital	1,000	1,000
Reinvested earnings	1,000	1,419
Total equity	2,050	2,469
Total liabilities and equity	8,750	9,869

DRILL 3 ▶
*Julie's boutiques,
continued*

Gross PP&E

Beg

Add

Sub

End

Accumulated Depr.

Beg

Add

Sub

End

Julie's Cash Flow Statement, continued

Cash flow statement	2001
Net income	
Depreciation	
(Increase) decrease in operating assets	
Increase (decrease) in operating liabilities	
Cash from operating activities	
Capital expenditure	
Sales of fixed assets	
(Increase) decrease in other assets	
Cash from investing activities	
Increase (decrease) in debt	
Increase (decrease) in cmn. stock & APIC	
Dividends	
Cash from financing activities	
Net cash flow	
Beginning cash balance from B/S	
Ending cash balance from B/S	
Difference	

Does Net cash flow = Difference? It should.

Bet's Burger Bars

Using the balance sheet and income statement for Bet's Burger Bars below calculate her cash flow statement. Use the BASE tables to help you. Assume:

- There were no sales of PP&E during the year.
- There were no purchases of intangibles during the year.

All figures in thousands

Income statement	2000	2001
Sales		89,000
COGS		(50,000)
Depreciation		(9,000)
Gross profit		30,000
SG&A		(8,900)
Amortization		(1,300)
Operating profit		19,800
Interest income		345
Interest expense		(3,487)
Profit before tax		16,658
Tax		(5,830)
Net income		10,828
Dividends		2,707

Balance sheet		
Assets		
Cash	1,437	5,017
Trade accounts receivable	26,700	35,000
Inventories	25,015	26,987
Prepaid expenses	2,500	2,645
Total current assets	55,652	69,649
Gross PP&E	78,920	79,420
Accumulated Depreciation	(45,652)	(54,652)
Net PP&E	33,268	24,768
Investments	3,697	2,540
Intangibles	8,975	7,675
Total assets	101,592	104,632
Liabilities		
Accounts payable & accrued expenses	21,458	25,897
Loans and notes payable	8.975	5,174
Total current liabilities	30,433	31,071
Long term debt	56,789	49.856
Total liabilities	87,222	80,927
Equity		
Common stock	125	128
Additional paid-in capital	5,648	6,859
Reinvested earnings	8,597	16,718
Total equity	14,370	23,705
Total liabilities and equity	101,592	104,632

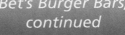

DRILL 4 ▶
Bet's Burger Bars, continued

Gross PP&E

Beg

Add

Sub

End

Accumulated Depr.

Beg

Add

Sub

End

Net intangibles

Beg

Add

Sub

End

Bet's Burger Bars, continued

Cash flow statement	2001
Net income	
Depreciation	
Amortization	
(Increase) decrease in operating assets	
Increase (decrease) in operating liabilities	
Cash from operating activities	
Capital expenditure	
Sales of fixed assets	
(Increase) decrease in other assets	
(Purchase) sale of Intangibles	
Cash from investing activities	
Increase (decrease) in debt	
Increase (decrease) in common stock & APIC	
Dividends	
Cash from financing activities	
Net cash flow	
Beginning cash balance from B/S	
Ending cash balance from B/S	
Difference	

Does Net cash flow = Difference? It should.

DRILL 5 ▶
The auction house

The Auction House

Julie Ann Ward owns a large auction house in Boston. Using her balance sheet and income statement below calculate her cash flow statement for 2001. Assume the following:

■ Her capital expenditure for the year was $12,760.

■ She sold some fixed assets for their book value (use the BASE tables to determine how much cash she received).

■ She did not sell any intangible assets.

All figures in thousands

Income statement	2000	2001
Sales		103,876
COGS		(81,265)
Depreciation		(8,756)
Gross profit		13,855
SG&A		(1,274)
Amortization		(908)
Operating profit		11,673
Interest income		3,456
Interest expense		(8,761)
Profit before tax		6,368
Tax		(2,229)
Net income		4,139
Dividends		1,345

Balance sheet	2000	2001
Assets		
Cash	64,141	52,321
Marketable securities	1,234	908
Trade accounts receivable	54,098	65,908
Inventories	34,567	32,196
Prepaid expenses	5,671	3,467
Total current assets	159,711	154,800
Gross PP&E	78,920	88,224
Accumulated Depreciation	(45,652)	(52,063)
Net PP&E	33,268	36,161
Investments	12,375	15,832
Intangibles	10,983	22,420
Total assets	216,337	229,213
Liabilities		
Accounts payable & accrued expenses	45,982	49,081
Loans and notes payable	34,093	26,092
Total current liabilities	80,075	75,173
Long term debt	109,234	123,098
Total liabilities	189,309	198,271
Equity		
Common stock	121	134
Additional paid-in capital	3,456	4,563
Reinvested earnings	23,451	26,245
Total equity	27,028	30,942
Total liabilities and equity	216,337	229,213

DRILL 4 ▶
The auction house, continued

Gross PP&E

Beg

Add

Sub

End

Accumulated Depr.

Beg

Add

Sub

End

Net intangibles

Beg

Add

Sub

End

The Auction House, continued

Cash flow statement	2001
Net income	
Depreciation	
Amortization	
(Increase) decrease in operating assets	
Increase (decrease) in operating liabilities	
Cash from operating activities	
Capital expenditure	
Sales of fixed assets	
(Increase) decrease in other assets	
(Purchase) sale of Intangibles	
Cash from investing activities	
Increase (decrease) in debt	
Increase (decrease) in common stock & APIC	
Dividends	
Cash from financing activities	
Net cash flow	
Beginning cash balance from B/S	
Ending cash balance from B/S	
Difference	

Does Net cash flow = Difference? It should.

2000 Coca-Cola Annual Report

Selected Financial Data

The Coca-Cola Company and Subsidiaries

(In millions except per share data, ratios and growth rates)	Compound Growth Rates		Year Ended December 31,	
	5 Years	10 Years	2000	1999
SUMMARY OF OPERATIONS				
Net operating revenues	2.4 %	7.1%	$ 20,458	$ 19,805
Cost of goods sold	(2.2)%	4.0%	6,204	6,009
Gross profit	5.0 %	8.9%	14,254	13,796
Selling, administrative and general expenses	5.2 %	8.4%	9,120	9,001
Other operating charges			1,443	813
Operating income	(1.7)%	6.6%	3,691	3,982
Interest income			345	260
Interest expense			447	337
Equity income (loss)			(289)	(184)
Other income (deductions)-net			99	98
Gains on issuances of stock by equity investees			—	—
Income from continuing operations before income taxes and changes in accounting principles	(4.7)%	5.4%	3,399	3,819
Income taxes	(1.9)%	6.8%	1,222	1,388
Income from continuing operations before changes in accounting principles	(6.1)%	4.6%	$ 2,177	$ 2,431
Net income	(6.1)%	4.6%	$ 2,177	$ 2,431
Preferred stock dividends			—	—
Net income available to common share owners	(6.1)%	4.8%	$ 2,177	$ 2,431
Average common shares outstanding			2,477	2,469
Average common shares outstanding assuming dilution			2,487	2,487
PER COMMON SHARE DATA				
Income from continuing operations before changes in accounting principles — basic	(5.7)%	5.6%	$ .88	$ .98
Income from continuing operations before changes in accounting principles — diluted	(5.5)%	5.8%	.88	.98
Basic net income	(5.7)%	5.6%	.88	.98
Diluted net income	(5.5)%	5.8%	.88	.98
Cash dividends	9.1 %	13.0%	.68	.64
Market price on December 31,	10.4 %	18.0%	60.94	58.25
TOTAL MARKET VALUE OF COMMON STOCK[1]	10.2 %	17.2%	$ 151,421	$ 143,969
BALANCE SHEET DATA				
Cash, cash equivalents and current marketable securities			$ 1,892	$ 1,812
Property, plant and equipment-net			4,168	4,267
Depreciation			465	438
Capital expenditures			733	1,069
Total assets			20,834	21,623
Long-term debt			835	854
Total debt			5,651	6,227
Share-owners' equity			9,316	9,513
Total capital [1]			14,967	15,740
OTHER KEY FINANCIAL MEASURES[1]				
Total debt-to-total capital			37.8%	39.6%
Net debt-to-net capital			29.4%	32.2%
Return on common equity			23.1%	27.1%
Return on capital			16.2%	18.2%
Dividend payout ratio			77.4%	65.0%
Free cash flow [7]			$ 2,806	$ 2,332
Economic profit			$ 861	$ 1,128

[1] See Glossary on page 73.

[2] In 1998, we adopted SFAS No. 132 "Employers' Disclosures about Pensions and Other Postretirement Benefits."

[3] In 1994, we adopted SFAS No. 115 "Accounting for Certain Investments in Debt and Equity Securities."

[4] In 1993, we adopted SFAS No. 112 "Employers' Accounting for Postemployment Benefits."

44

The Coca-Cola Company and Subsidiaries

1998[2]	1997[2]	1996[2]	1995[2]	1994[2,3]	1993[2,4]	1992[2,5,6]	1991[2,6]	1990[2,6]
$ 18,813	$ 18,868	$ 18,673	$ 18,127	$ 16,264	$ 14,030	$ 13,119	$ 11,599	$ 10,261
5,562	6,015	6,738	6,940	6,168	5,160	5,055	4,649	4,208
13,251	12,853	11,935	11,187	10,096	8,870	8,064	6,950	6,053
8,211	7,792	7,635	7,075	6,459	5,721	5,317	4,628	4,054
73	60	385	86	—	50	—	13	49
4,967	5,001	3,915	4,026	3,637	3,099	2,747	2,309	1,950
219	211	238	245	181	144	164	175	170
277	258	286	272	199	168	171	192	231
32	155	211	169	134	91	65	40	110
230	583	87	86	(25)	7	(59)	51	15
27	363	431	74	—	12	—	—	—
5,198	6,055	4,596	4,328	3,728	3,185	2,746	2,383	2,014
1,665	1,926	1,104	1,342	1,174	997	863	765	632
$ 3,533	$ 4,129	$ 3,492	$ 2,986	$ 2,554	$ 2,188	$ 1,883	$ 1,618	$ 1,382
$ 3,533	$ 4,129	$ 3,492	$ 2,986	$ 2,554	$ 2,176	$ 1,664	$ 1,618	$ 1,382
—	—	—	—	—	—	—	1	18
$ 3,533	$ 4,129	$ 3,492	$ 2,986	$ 2,554	$ 2,176	$ 1,664	$ 1,617	$ 1,364
2,467	2,477	2,494	2,525	2,580	2,603	2,634	2,666	2,674
2,496	2,515	2,523	2,549	2,599	2,626	2,668	2,695	2,706
$ 1.43	$ 1.67	$ 1.40	$ 1.18	$ .99	$ .84	$ .72	$ .61	$ .51
1.42	1.64	1.38	1.17	.98	.83	.71	.60	.50
1.43	1.67	1.40	1.18	.99	.84	.63	.61	.51
1.42	1.64	1.38	1.17	.98	.83	.62	.60	.50
.60	.56	.50	.44	.39	.34	.28	.24	.20
67.00	66.69	52.63	37.13	25.75	22.31	20.94	20.06	11.63
$ 165,190	$ 164,766	$ 130,575	$ 92,983	$ 65,711	$ 57,905	$ 54,728	$ 53,325	$ 31,073
$ 1,807	$ 1,843	$ 1,658	$ 1,315	$ 1,531	$ 1,078	$ 1,063	$ 1,117	$ 1,492
3,669	3,743	3,550	4,336	4,080	3,729	3,526	2,890	2,386
381	384	442	421	382	333	310	254	236
863	1,093	990	937	878	800	1,083	792	593
19,145	16,881	16,112	15,004	13,863	11,998	11,040	10,185	9,245
687	801	1,116	1,141	1,426	1,428	1,120	985	536
5,149	3,875	4,513	4,064	3,509	3,100	3,207	2,288	2,537
8,403	7,274	6,125	5,369	5,228	4,570	3,881	4,236	3,662
13,552	11,149	10,638	9,433	8,737	7,670	7,088	6,524	6,199
38.0 %	34.8 %	42.4 %	43.1 %	40.2 %	40.4 %	45.2 %	35.1 %	40.9 %
28.1 %	22.0 %	31.6 %	32.3 %	25.5 %	29.0 %	33.1 %	24.2 %	24.6 %
45.1 %	61.6 %	60.8 %	56.4 %	52.1 %	51.8 %	46.4 %	41.3 %	41.4 %
30.2 %	39.5 %	36.8 %	34.9 %	32.8 %	31.2 %	29.4 %	27.5 %	26.8 %
41.9 %	33.6 %	35.7 %	37.2 %	39.4 %	40.6 %	44.3 %	39.5 %	39.2 %
$ 1,876	$ 2,951	$ 2,215	$ 2,460	$ 2,356	$ 1,857	$ 875	$ 881	$ 844
$ 2,480	$ 3,325	$ 2,718	$ 2,291	$ 1,896	$ 1,549	$ 1,300	$ 1,073	$ 920

[5] In 1992, we adopted SFAS No. 106 "Employers' Accounting for Postretirement Benefits Other Than Pensions."

[6] In 1992, we adopted SFAS No. 109 "Accounting for Income Taxes," by restating financial statements beginning in 1989.

[7] All years presented have been restated to exclude net cash flows related to acquisitions.

45

Consolidated Balance Sheets

The Coca-Cola Company and Subsidiaries

December 31,	2000	1999
(In millions except share data)		
ASSETS		
CURRENT		
Cash and cash equivalents	$ 1,819	$ 1,611
Marketable securities	73	201
	1,892	1,812
Trade accounts receivable, less allowances		
of $62 in 2000 and $26 in 1999	1,757	1,798
Inventories	1,066	1,076
Prepaid expenses and other assets	1,905	1,794
TOTAL CURRENT ASSETS	6,620	6,480
INVESTMENTS AND OTHER ASSETS		
Equity method investments		
Coca-Cola Enterprises Inc.	707	728
Coca-Cola Amatil Limited	617	1,133
Coca-Cola HBC S.A.	758	788
Other, principally bottling companies	3,164	3,793
Cost method investments, principally bottling companies	519	350
Marketable securities and other assets	2,364	2,124
	8,129	8,916
PROPERTY, PLANT AND EQUIPMENT		
Land	225	215
Buildings and improvements	1,642	1,528
Machinery and equipment	4,547	4,527
Containers	200	201
	6,614	6,471
Less allowances for depreciation	2,446	2,204
	4,168	4,267
GOODWILL AND OTHER INTANGIBLE ASSETS	1,917	1,960
	$ 20,834	$ 21,623

46

The Coca-Cola Company and Subsidiaries

December 31,	2000	1999
LIABILITIES AND SHARE-OWNERS' EQUITY		
CURRENT		
Accounts payable and accrued expenses	$ 3,905	$ 3,714
Loans and notes payable	4,795	5,112
Current maturities of long-term debt	21	261
Accrued income taxes	600	769
TOTAL CURRENT LIABILITIES	9,321	9,856
LONG-TERM DEBT	835	854
OTHER LIABILITIES	1,004	902
DEFERRED INCOME TAXES	358	498
SHARE-OWNERS' EQUITY		
Common stock, $.25 par value		
Authorized: 5,600,000,000 shares		
Issued: 3,481,882,834 shares in 2000; 3,466,371,904 shares in 1999	870	867
Capital surplus	3,196	2,584
Reinvested earnings	21,265	20,773
Accumulated other comprehensive income and		
unearned compensation on restricted stock	(2,722)	(1,551)
	22,609	22,673
Less treasury stock, at cost (997,121,427 shares in 2000;		
994,796,786 shares in 1999)	13,293	13,160
	9,316	9,513
	$ 20,834	$ 21,623

See Notes to Consolidated Financial Statements.

47

Consolidated Statements of Income

The Coca-Cola Company and Subsidiaries

Year Ended December 31, (In millions except per share data)	2000	1999	1998
NET OPERATING REVENUES	$ 20,458	$ 19,805	$ 18,813
Cost of goods sold	6,204	6,009	5,562
GROSS PROFIT	14,254	13,796	13,251
Selling, administrative and general expenses	9,120	9,001	8,211
Other operating charges	1,443	813	73
OPERATING INCOME	3,691	3,982	4,967
Interest income	345	260	219
Interest expense	447	337	277
Equity income (loss)	(289)	(184)	32
Other income-net	99	98	230
Gains on issuances of stock by equity investees	—	—	27
INCOME BEFORE INCOME TAXES	3,399	3,819	5,198
Income taxes	1,222	1,388	1,665
NET INCOME	$ 2,177	$ 2,431	$ 3,533
BASIC NET INCOME PER SHARE	$ .88	$ .98	$ 1.43
DILUTED NET INCOME PER SHARE	$ .88	$ .98	$ 1.42
AVERAGE SHARES OUTSTANDING	2,477	2,469	2,467
Dilutive effect of stock options	10	18	29
AVERAGE SHARES OUTSTANDING ASSUMING DILUTION	2,487	2,487	2,496

See Notes to Consolidated Financial Statements.

Consolidated Statements of Cash Flows

The Coca-Cola Company and Subsidiaries

Year Ended December 31,	2000	1999	1998
(In millions)			
OPERATING ACTIVITIES			
Net income	$ 2,177	$ 2,431	$ 3,533
Depreciation and amortization	773	792	645
Deferred income taxes	3	97	(38)
Equity income or loss, net of dividends	380	292	31
Foreign currency adjustments	196	(41)	21
Gains on issuances of stock by equity investees	—	—	(27)
Gains on sales of assets, including bottling interests	(127)	(49)	(306)
Other operating charges	916	799	73
Other items	119	119	51
Net change in operating assets and liabilities	(852)	(557)	(550)
Net cash provided by operating activities	3,585	3,883	3,433
INVESTING ACTIVITIES			
Acquisitions and investments, principally trademarks and bottling companies	(397)	(1,876)	(1,428)
Purchases of investments and other assets	(508)	(518)	(610)
Proceeds from disposals of investments and other assets	290	176	1,036
Purchases of property, plant and equipment	(733)	(1,069)	(863)
Proceeds from disposals of property, plant and equipment	45	45	54
Other investing activities	138	(179)	(350)
Net cash used in investing activities	(1,165)	(3,421)	(2,161)
FINANCING ACTIVITIES			
Issuances of debt	3,671	3,411	1,818
Payments of debt	(4,256)	(2,455)	(410)
Issuances of stock	331	168	302
Purchases of stock for treasury	(133)	(15)	(1,563)
Dividends	(1,685)	(1,580)	(1,480)
Net cash used in financing activities	(2,072)	(471)	(1,333)
EFFECT OF EXCHANGE RATE CHANGES ON CASH AND CASH EQUIVALENTS	(140)	(28)	(28)
CASH AND CASH EQUIVALENTS			
Net increase (decrease) during the year	208	(37)	(89)
Balance at beginning of the year	1,611	1,648	1,737
Balance at end of year	$ 1,819	$ 1,611	$ 1,648

See Notes to Consolidated Financial Statements.

Consolidated Statements of Share-Owners' Equity

The Coca-Cola Company and Subsidiaries

Three Years Ended December 31, 2000 (In millions except per share data)	Number of Common Shares Outstanding	Common Stock	Capital Surplus	Reinvested Earnings	Outstanding Restricted Stock	Accumulated Other Comprehensive Income	Treasury Stock	Total
BALANCE DECEMBER 31, 1997	2,471	$ 861	$ 1,527	$ 17,869	$ (50)	$ (1,351)	$ (11,582)	$ 7,274
Comprehensive income:								
Net income	—	—	—	3,533	—	—	—	3,533
Translation adjustments	—	—	—	—	—	52	—	52
Net change in unrealized gain on securities	—	—	—	—	—	(47)	—	(47)
Minimum pension liability	—	—	—	—	—	(4)	—	(4)
Comprehensive income								3,534
Stock issued to employees exercising stock options	16	4	298	—	—	—	—	302
Tax benefit from employees' stock option and restricted stock plans	—	—	97	—	—	—	—	97
Stock issued under restricted stock plans, less amortization of $5	1	—	47	—	(34)	—	—	13
Stock issued by an equity investee	—	—	226	—	—	—	—	226
Purchases of stock for treasury	(22)[1]	—	—	—	—	—	(1,563)	(1,563)
Dividends (per share — $.60)	—	—	—	(1,480)	—	—	—	(1,480)
BALANCE DECEMBER 31, 1998	2,466	865	2,195	19,922	(84)	(1,350)	(13,145)	8,403
Comprehensive income:								
Net income	—	—	—	2,431	—	—	—	2,431
Translation adjustments	—	—	—	—	—	(190)	—	(190)
Net change in unrealized gain on securities	—	—	—	—	—	23	—	23
Minimum pension liability	—	—	—	—	—	25	—	25
Comprehensive income								2,289
Stock issued to employees exercising stock options	6	2	166	—	—	—	—	168
Tax benefit from employees' stock option and restricted stock plans	—	—	72	—	—	—	—	72
Stock issued under restricted stock plans, less amortization of $27	—	—	2	—	25	—	—	27
Stock issued by an equity investee	—	—	146	—	—	—	—	146
Stock issued under Directors' plan	—	—	3	—	—	—	—	3
Purchases of stock for treasury	—	—	—	—	—	—	(15)	(15)
Dividends (per share — $.64)	—	—	—	(1,580)	—	—	—	(1,580)
BALANCE DECEMBER 31, 1999	2,472	867	2,584	20,773	(59)	(1,492)	(13,160)	9,513
Comprehensive income:								
Net income	—	—	—	2,177	—	—	—	2,177
Translation adjustments	—	—	—	—	—	(965)	—	(965)
Net change in unrealized gain on securities	—	—	—	—	—	(60)	—	(60)
Minimum pension liability	—	—	—	—	—	(10)	—	(10)
Comprehensive income								1,142
Stock issued to employees exercising stock options	12	2	329	—	—	—	—	331
Tax benefit from employees' stock option and restricted stock plans	—	—	116	—	—	—	—	116
Stock issued under restricted stock plans, less amortization of $24	3	1	166	—	(136)	—	—	31
Stock issued under Directors' plan	—	—	1	—	—	—	—	1
Purchases of stock for treasury	(2)[1]	—	—	—	—	—	(133)	(133)
Dividends (per share — $.68)	—	—	—	(1,685)	—	—	—	(1,685)
BALANCE DECEMBER 31, 2000	2,485	$ 870	$ 3,196	$ 21,265	$ (195)	$ (2,527)	$ (13,293)	$ 9,316

[1] Common stock purchased from employees exercising stock options numbered 2.2 million, .3 million and 1.4 million shares for the years ended December 31, 2000, 1999 and 1998, respectively.

See Notes to Consolidated Financial Statements.

50

Notes to Consolidated Financial Statements

The Coca-Cola Company and Subsidiaries

NOTE 1: ORGANIZATION AND SUMMARY OF SIGNIFICANT ACCOUNTING POLICIES

Organization

The Coca-Cola Company and subsidiaries (our Company) is predominantly a manufacturer, marketer and distributor of nonalcoholic beverage concentrates and syrups. Operating in nearly 200 countries worldwide, we primarily sell our concentrates and syrups to bottling and canning operations, fountain wholesalers and fountain retailers. We also market and distribute juice and juice-drink products. We have significant markets for our products in all the world's geographic regions. We record revenue when title passes to our customers or our bottling partners.

Basis of Presentation

Certain amounts in the prior years' financial statements have been reclassified to conform to the current year presentation.

Consolidation

Our Consolidated Financial Statements include the accounts of The Coca-Cola Company and all subsidiaries except where control is temporary or does not rest with our Company. Our investments in companies in which we have the ability to exercise significant influence over operating and financial policies, including certain investments where there is a temporary majority interest, are accounted for by the equity method. Accordingly, our Company's share of the net earnings of these companies is included in consolidated net income. Our investments in other companies are carried at cost or fair value, as appropriate. All significant intercompany accounts and transactions are eliminated upon consolidation.

Issuances of Stock by Equity Investees

When one of our equity investees issues additional shares to third parties, our percentage ownership interest in the investee decreases. In the event the issuance price per share is more or less than our average carrying amount per share, we recognize a noncash gain or loss on the issuance. This noncash gain or loss, net of any deferred taxes, is generally recognized in our net income in the period the change of ownership interest occurs.

If gains have been previously recognized on issuances of an equity investee's stock and shares of the equity investee are subsequently repurchased by the equity investee, gain recognition does not occur on issuances subsequent to the date of a repurchase until shares have been issued in an amount equivalent to the number of repurchased shares. This type of transaction is reflected as an equity transaction and the net effect is reflected in the accompanying Consolidated Balance Sheets. For specific transaction details, refer to Note 3.

Advertising Costs

Our Company expenses production costs of print, radio and television advertisements as of the first date the advertisements take place. Advertising expenses included in selling, administrative and general expenses were $1,742 million in 2000, $1,699 million in 1999 and $1,597 million in 1998. As of December 31, 2000 and 1999, advertising costs of approximately $818 million and $523 million, respectively, were recorded primarily in prepaid expenses and other assets and in marketable securities and other assets in the accompanying Consolidated Balance Sheets.

Net Income Per Share

Basic net income per share is computed by dividing net income by the weighted-average number of shares outstanding. Diluted net income per share includes the dilutive effect of stock options.

Cash Equivalents

Marketable securities that are highly liquid and have maturities of three months or less at the date of purchase are classified as cash equivalents.

Inventories

Inventories consist primarily of raw materials and supplies and are valued at the lower of cost or market. In general, cost is determined on the basis of average cost or first-in, first-out methods.

Property, Plant and Equipment

Property, plant and equipment are stated at cost and are depreciated principally by the straight-line method over the estimated useful lives of the assets.

Other Assets

Our Company invests in infrastructure programs with our bottlers that are directed at strengthening our bottling system and increasing unit case sales. The costs of these programs are recorded in other assets and are subsequently amortized over the periods to be directly benefited.

Goodwill and Other Intangible Assets

Goodwill and other intangible assets are stated on the basis of cost and are amortized, principally on a straight-line basis, over the estimated future periods to be benefited (not exceeding 40 years). Goodwill and other intangible assets are periodically reviewed for impairment to ensure they are appropriately valued. Conditions that may indicate an impairment issue exists include an economic downturn in a worldwide market or a change in the assessment of future operations. In the event that a condition is identified that may indicate an impairment issue exists, an assessment is performed using a variety of methodologies, including cash flow analysis, estimates of sales proceeds and independent appraisals. Where

51

Notes to Consolidated Financial Statements

The Coca-Cola Company and Subsidiaries

applicable, an appropriate interest rate is utilized, based on location-specific economic factors. Accumulated amortization was approximately $192 million and $154 million on December 31, 2000 and 1999, respectively.

Use of Estimates

In conformity with generally accepted accounting principles, the preparation of our financial statements requires our management to make estimates and assumptions that affect the amounts reported in our financial statements and accompanying notes including our assessment of the carrying value of our investments in bottling operations. Although these estimates are based on our knowledge of current events and actions we may undertake in the future, actual results may ultimately differ from estimates.

New Accounting Standards

In June 1998, the Financial Accounting Standards Board issued Statement of Financial Accounting Standards (SFAS) No. 133, "Accounting for Derivative Instruments and Hedging Activities," as amended by Statements 137 and 138 in June 1999 and June 2000, respectively. These statements, which were required to be adopted for fiscal years beginning after June 15, 2000, require the Company to recognize all derivatives on the balance sheet at fair value. The statements also established new accounting rules for hedging instruments which, depending on the nature of the hedge, require that changes in the fair value of derivatives either be offset against the change in fair value of assets, liabilities or firm commitments through earnings, or be recognized in other comprehensive income until the hedged item is recognized in earnings. Any ineffective portion of a derivative's change in fair value must be immediately recognized in earnings.

We adopted the provisions of SFAS No. 133, as amended, on January 1, 2001, which resulted in an immaterial impact on our consolidated results of operations and financial position. Although these statements will not have a material impact in our annual consolidated financial results, the requirements of these statements may result in slightly increased volatility in the Company's future quarterly consolidated financial results. The Company implemented new information systems to ensure that we were in compliance with these statements upon adoption.

NOTE 2: BOTTLING INVESTMENTS

Coca-Cola Enterprises Inc.

Coca-Cola Enterprises is the largest soft-drink bottler in the world, operating in eight countries, and is one of our anchor bottlers. On December 31, 2000, our Company owned approximately 40 percent of the outstanding common stock of Coca-Cola Enterprises, and accordingly, we account for our investment by the equity method of accounting. The excess of our equity in the underlying net assets of Coca-Cola Enterprises over our investment is primarily amortized on

a straight-line basis over 40 years. The balance of this excess, net of amortization, was approximately $438 million on December 31, 2000. A summary of financial information for Coca-Cola Enterprises is as follows (in millions):

December 31,	2000	1999
Current assets	$ 2,631	$ 2,581
Noncurrent assets	19,531	20,149
Total assets	$ 22,162	$ 22,730
Current liabilities	$ 3,094	$ 3,614
Noncurrent liabilities	16,234	16,192
Total liabilities	$ 19,328	$ 19,806
Share-owners' equity	$ 2,834	$ 2,924
Company equity investment	$ 707	$ 728

Year Ended December 31,	2000	1999	1998
Net operating revenues	$ 14,750	$ 14,406	$ 13,414
Cost of goods sold	9,083	9,015	8,391
Gross profit	$ 5,667	$ 5,391	$ 5,023
Operating income	$ 1,126	$ 839	$ 869
Cash operating profit[1]	$ 2,387	$ 2,187	$ 1,989
Net income	$ 236	$ 59	$ 142
Net income available to common share owners	$ 233	$ 56	$ 141

[1] Cash operating profit is defined as operating income plus depreciation expense, amortization expense and other noncash operating expenses.

Our net concentrate and syrup sales to Coca-Cola Enterprises were $3.5 billion in 2000, $3.3 billion in 1999 and $3.1 billion in 1998, or approximately 17 percent, 17 percent and 16 percent of our 2000, 1999 and 1998 net operating revenues, respectively. Coca-Cola Enterprises purchases sweeteners through our Company; however, related collections from Coca-Cola Enterprises and payments to suppliers are not included in our Consolidated Statements of Income. These transactions amounted to $298 million in 2000, $308 million in 1999 and $252 million in 1998. We also provide certain administrative and other services to Coca-Cola Enterprises under negotiated fee arrangements.

Our direct support for certain marketing activities of Coca-Cola Enterprises and participation with them in cooperative advertising and other marketing programs amounted to approximately $766 million in 2000, $767 million in 1999 and $899 million in 1998. Pursuant to cooperative advertising and trade arrangements with Coca-Cola Enterprises, we received approximately $195 million, $243 million and $173 million in 2000, 1999 and 1998, respectively, from Coca-Cola Enterprises for local media and marketing program expense reimbursements. Additionally, we committed approximately $223 million in 2000, $338 million in 1999 and $324 million in 1998, respectively, to Coca-Cola Enterprises under a Company program that encourages bottlers to invest in building and supporting beverage infrastructure.

52

Notes to Consolidated Financial Statements
The Coca-Cola Company and Subsidiaries

If valued at the December 31, 2000, quoted closing price of publicly traded Coca-Cola Enterprises shares, the calculated value of our investment in Coca-Cola Enterprises would have exceeded its carrying value by approximately $2.5 billion.

Other Equity Investments
Operating results include our proportionate share of income (loss) from our equity investments. A summary of financial information for our equity investments in the aggregate, other than Coca-Cola Enterprises, is as follows (in millions):

December 31,	2000	1999
Current assets	$ 5,985	$ 6,652
Noncurrent assets	19,030	21,306
Total assets	$ 25,015	$ 27,958
Current liabilities	$ 5,419	$ 6,550
Noncurrent liabilities	8,357	8,361
Total liabilities	$ 13,776	$ 14,911
Share-owners' equity	$ 11,239	$ 13,047
Company equity investment	$ 4,539	$ 5,714

Year Ended December 31,	2000	1999	1998
Net operating revenues	$ 21,666	$ 19,785	$ 17,975
Cost of goods sold	13,014	12,085	11,122
Gross profit	$ 8,652	$ 7,700	$ 6,853
Operating income (loss)	$ (24)	$ 809	$ 905
Cash operating profit[1]	$ 2,796	$ 2,474	$ 1,998
Net income (loss)	$ (894)	$ (134)	$ 217

Equity investments include certain nonbottling investees.

[1] Cash operating profit is defined as operating income plus depreciation expense, amortization expense and other noncash operating expenses.

Net sales to equity investees other than Coca-Cola Enterprises were $3.5 billion in 2000, $3.2 billion in 1999 and $2.6 billion in 1998. Our direct support for certain marketing activities with equity investees other than Coca-Cola Enterprises, the majority of which are located outside the United States, was approximately $663 million, $685 million and $640 million for 2000, 1999 and 1998, respectively.

In July 1999, we acquired from Fraser and Neave Limited its ownership interest in F&N Coca-Cola as discussed in Note 17. In August 1998, we exchanged our Korean bottling operations with Coca-Cola Amatil for an additional ownership interest in Coca-Cola Amatil.

In June 1998, we sold our previously consolidated Italian bottling and canning operations to Coca-Cola Beverages. This transaction resulted in proceeds valued at approximately $1.0 billion and an after-tax gain of approximately $.03 per share (basic and diluted).

If valued at the December 31, 2000, quoted closing prices of shares actively traded on stock markets, the calculated value of our equity investments in publicly traded bottlers other than Coca-Cola Enterprises would have exceeded our carrying value by approximately $1.0 billion.

NOTE 3: ISSUANCES OF STOCK BY EQUITY INVESTEES
No gains on issuances of stock by equity investees were recorded during 2000. In the first quarter of 1999, Coca-Cola Enterprises completed its acquisition of various bottlers. These transactions were funded primarily with shares of Coca-Cola Enterprises common stock. The Coca-Cola Enterprises common stock issued was valued in an amount greater than the book value per share of our investment in Coca-Cola Enterprises. As a result of these transactions, our equity in the underlying net assets of Coca-Cola Enterprises increased, and we recorded a $241 million increase to our Company's investment basis in Coca-Cola Enterprises. Due to Coca-Cola Enterprises' share repurchase program, the increase in our investment in Coca-Cola Enterprises was recorded as an equity transaction, and no gain was recognized. We recorded a deferred tax liability of approximately $95 million on this increase to our investment in Coca-Cola Enterprises. These transactions reduced our ownership in Coca-Cola Enterprises from approximately 42 percent to approximately 40 percent.

In December 1998, Coca-Cola Enterprises completed its acquisition of certain independent bottling operations operating in parts of Texas, New Mexico and Arizona (collectively known as the Wolslager Group). The transactions were funded primarily with the issuance of shares of Coca-Cola Enterprises common stock. The Coca-Cola Enterprises common stock issued in exchange for these bottlers was valued at an amount greater than the book value per share of our investment in Coca-Cola Enterprises. As a result of this transaction, our equity in the underlying net assets of Coca-Cola Enterprises increased, and we recorded a $116 million increase to our Company's investment basis in Coca-Cola Enterprises. Due to Coca-Cola Enterprises' share repurchase program the increase in our investment in Coca-Cola Enterprises was recorded as an equity transaction, and no gain was recognized. We recorded a deferred tax liability of approximately $46 million on this increase to our investment in Coca-Cola Enterprises. At the completion of this transaction, our ownership in Coca-Cola Enterprises was approximately 42 percent.

In September 1998, CCEAG, our bottler in Germany, issued new shares valued at approximately $275 million to effect a merger with Nordwest Getränke GmbH & Co. KG, another German bottler. Approximately 7.5 million shares were issued, resulting in a one-time noncash pretax gain for our Company of approximately $27 million. We provided deferred taxes of approximately $10 million on this gain. This issuance reduced our ownership in CCEAG from approximately 45 percent to approximately 40 percent.

In June 1998, Coca-Cola Enterprises completed its acquisition of CCBG Corporation and Texas Bottling Group, Inc. (collectively known as Coke Southwest). The transaction was valued at approximately $1.1 billion. Approximately 55 percent of the transaction was funded with the issuance of approximately 17.7 million shares of Coca-Cola Enterprises common stock, and the remaining portion was funded through debt and assumed debt. The

Notes to Consolidated Financial Statements
The Coca-Cola Company and Subsidiaries

Coca-Cola Enterprises common stock issued in exchange for Coke Southwest was valued at an amount greater than the book value per share of our investment in Coca-Cola Enterprises. As a result of this transaction, our equity in the underlying net assets of Coca-Cola Enterprises increased and we recorded a $257 million increase to our Company's investment basis in Coca-Cola Enterprises. Due to Coca-Cola Enterprises' share repurchase program, the increase in our investment in Coca-Cola Enterprises was recorded as an equity transaction, and no gain was recognized. We recorded a deferred tax liability of approximately $101 million on this increase to our investment in Coca-Cola Enterprises. At the completion of this transaction, our ownership in Coca-Cola Enterprises was approximately 42 percent.

NOTE 4: ACCOUNTS PAYABLE AND ACCRUED EXPENSES

Accounts payable and accrued expenses consist of the following (in millions):

December 31,	2000	1999
Accrued marketing	$ 1,163	$ 1,056
Container deposits	58	53
Accrued compensation	141	164
Sales, payroll and other taxes	166	297
Accrued realignment expenses	254	—
Accounts payable and other accrued expenses	2,123	2,144
	$ 3,905	$ 3,714

NOTE 5: SHORT-TERM BORROWINGS AND CREDIT ARRANGEMENTS

Loans and notes payable consist primarily of commercial paper issued in the United States. On December 31, 2000, we had $4.5 billion outstanding in commercial paper borrowings. In addition, we had $3.0 billion in lines of credit and other short-term credit facilities available, of which approximately $246 million was outstanding. Our weighted-average interest rates for commercial paper outstanding were approximately 6.7 percent and 6.0 percent at December 31, 2000 and 1999, respectively.

These facilities are subject to normal banking terms and conditions. Some of the financial arrangements require compensating balances, none of which is presently significant to our Company.

NOTE 6: LONG-TERM DEBT

Long-term debt consists of the following (in millions):

December 31,	2000	1999
6% U.S. dollar notes due 2000	$ —	$ 250
6 5/8% U.S. dollar notes due 2002	150	150
6% U.S. dollar notes due 2003	150	150
5 3/4% U.S. dollar notes due 2009	399	399
7 3/8% U.S. dollar notes due 2093	116	116
Other, due 2001 to 2013	41	50
	856	1,115
Less current portion	21	261
	$ 835	$ 854

After giving effect to interest rate management instruments, the principal amount of our long-term debt that had fixed and variable interest rates, respectively, was $706 million and $150 million on December 31, 2000, and $690 million and $425 million on December 31, 1999. The weighted-average interest rate on our Company's long-term debt was 5.9 percent and 5.6 percent for the years ended December 31, 2000 and 1999, respectively. Total interest paid was approximately $458 million, $314 million and $298 million in 2000, 1999 and 1998, respectively. For a more complete discussion of interest rate management, refer to Note 9.

Maturities of long-term debt for the five years succeeding December 31, 2000, are as follows (in millions):

2001	2002	2003	2004	2005
$ 21	$ 154	$ 153	$ 2	$ 1

The above notes include various restrictions, none of which is presently significant to our Company.

NOTE 7: COMPREHENSIVE INCOME

Accumulated other comprehensive income consists of the following (in millions):

December 31,	2000	1999
Foreign currency translation adjustment	$ (2,475)	$ (1,510)
Unrealized gain on available-for-sale securities	(26)	34
Minimum pension liability	(26)	(16)
	$ (2,527)	$ (1,492)

Notes to Consolidated Financial Statements

The Coca-Cola Company and Subsidiaries

A summary of the components of other comprehensive income for the years ended December 31, 2000, 1999 and 1998, is as follows (in millions):

December 31, 2000	Before-Tax Amount	Income Tax	After-Tax Amount
Net foreign currency translation	$ (1,074)	$ 109	$ (965)
Net change in unrealized gain (loss) on available-for-sale securities	(90)	30	(60)
Minimum pension liability	(17)	7	(10)
Other comprehensive income (loss)	$ (1,181)	$ 146	$ (1,035)

December 31, 1999	Before-Tax Amount	Income Tax	After-Tax Amount
Net foreign currency translation	$ (249)	$ 59	$ (190)
Net change in unrealized gain (loss) on available-for-sale securities	37	(14)	23
Minimum pension liability	38	(13)	25
Other comprehensive income (loss)	$ (174)	$ 32	$ (142)

December 31, 1998	Before-Tax Amount	Income Tax	After-Tax Amount
Net foreign currency translation	$ 52	$ —	$ 52
Net change in unrealized gain (loss) on available-for-sale securities	(70)	23	(47)
Minimum pension liability	(5)	1	(4)
Other comprehensive income (loss)	$ (23)	$ 24	$ 1

NOTE 8: FINANCIAL INSTRUMENTS

Fair Value of Financial Instruments

The carrying amounts reflected in our Consolidated Balance Sheets for cash, cash equivalents, marketable equity securities, cost method investments, receivables, loans and notes payable and long-term debt approximate their respective fair values. Fair values are based primarily on quoted prices for those or similar instruments. A comparison of the carrying value and fair value of our hedging instruments is included in Note 9.

Certain Debt and Marketable Equity Securities

Investments in debt and marketable equity securities, other than investments accounted for by the equity method, are categorized as either trading, available-for-sale or held-to-maturity. On December 31, 2000 and 1999, we had no trading securities. Securities categorized as available-for-sale are stated at fair value, with unrealized gains and losses, net of deferred income taxes, reported as a component of accumulated other comprehensive income. Debt securities categorized as held-to-maturity are stated at amortized cost.

On December 31, 2000 and 1999, available-for-sale and held-to-maturity securities consisted of the following (in millions):

December 31, 2000	Cost	Gross Unrealized Gains	Gross Unrealized Losses	Estimated Fair Value
Available-for-sale securities				
Equity securities	$ 248	$ 57	$ (90)	$ 215
Collateralized mortgage obligations	25	—	(2)	23
Other debt securities	15	—	—	15
	$ 288	$ 57	$ (92)	$ 253
Held-to-maturity securities				
Bank and corporate debt	$ 1,115	$ —	$ —	$ 1,115
	$ 1,115	$ —	$ —	$ 1,115

Notes to Consolidated Financial Statements

The Coca-Cola Company and Subsidiaries

December 31,	Cost	Gross Unrealized Gains	Gross Unrealized Losses	Estimated Fair Value
1999				
Available-for-sale securities				
Equity securities	$ 246	$ 69	$ (13)	$ 302
Collateralized mortgage obligations	45	—	(1)	44
Other debt securities	8	—	—	8
	$ 299	$ 69	$ (14)	$ 354
Held-to-maturity securities				
Bank and corporate debt	$ 1,137	$ —	$ —	$ 1,137
Other debt securities	49	—	—	49
	$ 1,186	$ —	$ —	$ 1,186

On December 31, 2000 and 1999, these investments were included in the following captions in our Consolidated Balance Sheets (in millions):

December 31,	Available-for-Sale Securities	Held-to-Maturity Securities
2000		
Cash and cash equivalents	$ —	$1,113
Current marketable securities	71	2
Cost method investments, principally bottling companies	151	—
Marketable securities and other assets	31	—
	$253	$1,115
1999		
Cash and cash equivalents	$ —	$ 1,061
Current marketable securities	76	125
Cost method investments, principally bottling companies	227	—
Marketable securities and other assets	51	—
	$ 354	$ 1,186

The contractual maturities of these investments as of December 31, 2000, were as follows (in millions):

	Available-for-Sale Securities		Held-to-Maturity Securities	
	Cost	Fair Value	Amortized Cost	Fair Value
2001	$ 7	$ 7	$ 1,115	$ 1,115
2002–2005	8	8	—	—
Collateralized mortgage obligations	25	23	—	—
Equity securities	248	215	—	—
	$ 288	$ 253	$ 1,115	$ 1,115

For the years ended December 31, 2000 and 1999, gross realized gains and losses on sales of available-for-sale securities were not material. The cost of securities sold is based on the specific identification method.

NOTE 9: HEDGING TRANSACTIONS AND DERIVATIVE FINANCIAL INSTRUMENTS

Our Company uses derivative financial instruments primarily to reduce our exposure to adverse fluctuations in interest rates and foreign exchange rates and, to a lesser extent, to reduce our exposure to adverse fluctuations in commodity prices and other market risks. When entered into, these financial instruments are designated as hedges of underlying exposures. Because of the high correlation between the hedging instrument and the underlying exposure being hedged, fluctuations in the value of the instruments are generally offset by changes in the value of the underlying exposures. Virtually all our derivatives are "over-the-counter" instruments. Our Company does not enter into derivative financial instruments for trading purposes.

The estimated fair values of derivatives used to hedge or modify our risks fluctuate over time. These fair value amounts should not be viewed in isolation, but rather in relation to the fair values of the underlying hedging transactions and investments and to the overall reduction in our exposure to adverse fluctuations in interest rates, foreign exchange rates, commodity prices and other market risks.

The notional amounts of the derivative financial instruments do not necessarily represent amounts exchanged by the parties and, therefore, are not a direct measure of our exposure from our use of derivatives. The amounts exchanged are calculated by reference to the notional amounts and by other terms of the derivatives, such as interest rates, exchange rates or other financial indices.

We have established strict counterparty credit guidelines and enter into transactions only with financial institutions of investment grade or better. We monitor counterparty exposures daily and review any downgrade in credit rating immediately. If a downgrade in the credit rating of a counterparty were to occur, we have provisions requiring

56

Notes to Consolidated Financial Statements

The Coca-Cola Company and Subsidiaries

collateral in the form of U.S. government securities for substantially all our transactions. To mitigate presettlement risk, minimum credit standards become more stringent as the duration of the derivative financial instrument increases. To minimize the concentration of credit risk, we enter into derivative transactions with a portfolio of financial institutions. As a result, we consider the risk of counterparty default to be minimal.

Interest Rate Management

Our Company maintains a percentage of fixed and variable rate debt within defined parameters. We enter into interest rate swap agreements that maintain the fixed-to-variable mix within these parameters. These contracts had maturities ranging from one to four years on December 31, 2000. Variable rates are predominantly linked to the London Interbank Offered Rate. Any differences paid or received on interest rate swap agreements are recognized as adjustments to interest expense over the life of each swap, thereby adjusting the effective interest rate on the underlying obligation. Additionally, our Company enters into interest rate cap agreements that may entitle us to receive from a financial institution the amount, if any, by which our interest payments on our variable rate debt exceed prespecified interest rates through 2004.

Foreign Currency Management

The purpose of our foreign currency hedging activities is to reduce the risk that our eventual dollar net cash inflows resulting from sales outside the United States will be adversely affected by changes in exchange rates.

We enter into forward exchange contracts and purchase currency options (principally Euro and Japanese yen) to hedge firm sale commitments denominated in foreign currencies. We also purchase currency options (principally Euro and Japanese yen) to hedge certain anticipated sales. Premiums paid and realized gains and losses, including those on any terminated contracts, are included in prepaid expenses and other assets. These are recognized in income, along with unrealized gains and losses in the same period the hedging transactions are realized. Approximately $26 million of realized gains and $85 million of realized losses on settled contracts entered into as hedges of firmly committed transactions that have not yet occurred were deferred on December 31, 2000 and 1999, respectively. Deferred gains/losses from hedging anticipated transactions were not material on December 31, 2000 or 1999. In the unlikely event that the underlying transaction terminates or becomes improbable, the deferred gains or losses on the associated derivative will be recorded in our income statement.

Gains and losses on derivative financial instruments that are designated and effective as hedges of net investments in international operations are included in share-owners' equity as a foreign currency translation adjustment, a component of accumulated other comprehensive income.

The following tables present the aggregate notional principal amounts, carrying values, fair values and maturities of our derivative financial instruments outstanding on December 31, 2000 and 1999 (in millions):

December 31,	Notional Principal Amounts	Carrying Values	Fair Values	Maturity
2000				
Interest rate management				
Swap agreements				
Assets	$ 150	$ 1	$ 8	2003
Liabilities	25	(1)	(10)	2001-2003
Interest rate caps				
Assets	1,600	8	4	2004
Foreign currency management				
Forward contracts				
Assets	1,812	49	74	2001
Swap agreements				
Assets	48	2	(3)	2001
Liabilities	359	(2)	(19)	2001-2002
Purchased options				
Assets	706	18	53	2001-2002
Other				
Assets	87	2	3	2001
	$ 4,787	$ 77	$ 110	

Notes to Consolidated Financial Statements
The Coca-Cola Company and Subsidiaries

December 31, 1999	Notional Principal Amounts	Carrying Values	Fair Values	Maturity
Interest rate management				
Swap agreements				
Assets	$ 250	$ 2	$ 6	2000-2003
Liabilities	200	(1)	(8)	2000-2003
Foreign currency management				
Forward contracts				
Assets	1,108	57	71	2000-2001
Liabilities	344	(6)	(3)	2000-2001
Swap agreements				
Assets	102	9	16	2000
Liabilities	412	—	(77)	2000-2002
Purchased options				
Assets	1,770	47	18	2000
Other				
Assets	185	—	2	2000
Liabilities	126	(8)	(8)	2000
	$ 4,497	$ 100	$ 17	

Maturities of derivative financial instruments held on December 31, 2000, are as follows (in millions):

2001	2002	2003	2004
$ 2,878	$ 234	$ 75	$ 1,600

NOTE 10: COMMITMENTS AND CONTINGENCIES

On December 31, 2000, we were contingently liable for guarantees of indebtedness owed by third parties in the amount of $397 million, of which $7 million related to independent bottling licensees. We do not consider it probable that we will be required to satisfy these guarantees.

We believe our exposure to concentrations of credit risk is limited, due to the diverse geographic areas covered by our operations.

We have committed to make future marketing expenditures of $772 million, of which the majority is payable over the next 12 years. Additionally, under certain circumstances, we have committed to make future investments in bottling companies. However, we do not consider any of these commitments to be individually significant.

NOTE 11: NET CHANGE IN OPERATING ASSETS AND LIABILITIES

The changes in operating assets and liabilities, net of effects of acquisitions and divestitures of businesses and unrealized exchange gains/losses, are as follows (in millions):

	2000	1999	1998
Increase in trade accounts receivable	$ (39)	$ (96)	$ (237)
Increase in inventories	(2)	(163)	(12)
Increase in prepaid expenses and other assets	(618)	(547)	(318)
Increase (decrease) in accounts payable and accrued expenses	(84)	281	(70)
Increase (decrease) in accrued taxes	(96)	(36)	120
Increase (decrease) in other liabilities	(13)	4	(33)
	$ (852)	$ (557)	$ (550)

NOTE 12: RESTRICTED STOCK, STOCK OPTIONS AND OTHER STOCK PLANS

Our Company currently sponsors restricted stock award plans and stock option plans. Our Company applies Accounting Principles Board Opinion No. 25 and related Interpretations in accounting for our plans. Accordingly, no compensation cost has been recognized for our stock option plans. The compensation cost charged against income for our restricted stock award plans was $6 million in 2000, $39 million in 1999 and $14 million in 1998. In addition, the Company recorded a charge of $37 million for special termination benefits as part of the Realignment discussed in Note 16. Had compensation cost for the stock option plans been determined based on the fair value at the grant dates for awards under the plans, our Company's net income and net income per share (basic and diluted) would have been as presented in the following table.

58

Notes to Consolidated Financial Statements
The Coca-Cola Company and Subsidiaries

The pro forma amounts are indicated below (in millions, except per share amounts):

Year Ended December 31,	2000	1999	1998
Net income			
As reported	$ 2,177	$ 2,431	$ 3,533
Pro forma	$ 1,995	$ 2,271	$ 3,405
Basic net income per share			
As reported	$ .88	$ .98	$ 1.43
Pro forma	$ .81	$ .92	$ 1.38
Diluted net income per share			
As reported	$ .88	$ .98	$ 1.42
Pro forma	$ .80	$ .91	$ 1.36

Under the amended 1989 Restricted Stock Award Plan and the amended 1983 Restricted Stock Award Plan (the Restricted Stock Award Plans), 40 million and 24 million shares of restricted common stock, respectively, may be granted to certain officers and key employees of our Company.

On December 31, 2000, 30 million shares were available for grant under the Restricted Stock Award Plans. In 2000, there were 546,585 shares of restricted stock granted at an average price of $58.20. In 1999, there were 32,100 shares of restricted stock granted at an average price of $53.86. In 1998, 707,300 shares of restricted stock were granted at an average price of $67.03. Participants are entitled to vote and receive dividends on the shares and, under the 1983 Restricted Stock Award Plan, participants are reimbursed by our Company for income taxes imposed on the award, but not for taxes generated by the reimbursement payment. The shares are subject to certain transfer restrictions and may be forfeited if a participant leaves our Company for reasons other than retirement, disability or death, absent a change in control of our Company.

In addition, 270,000 shares of three-year performance-based and 2,025,000 shares of five-year performance-based restricted stock were granted in 2000. The release of these shares is contingent upon the Company achieving certain predefined performance targets over the three-year or five-year measurement periods, respectively. Participants are entitled to vote and receive dividends on these shares during the measurement period. The Company also promised to grant 180,000 shares of stock at the end of three years and 200,000 shares of stock at the end of five years to certain employees if the Company achieves predefined performance targets over the three-year or five-year periods, respectively. The Company did not grant any performance-based stock awards in 1999 or 1998.

Under our 1991 Stock Option Plan (the 1991 Option Plan), a maximum of 120 million shares of our common stock was approved to be issued or transferred to certain officers and employees pursuant to stock options and stock appreciation rights granted under the 1991 Option Plan. The stock appreciation rights permit the holder, upon surrendering all or part of the related stock option,

to receive cash, common stock or a combination thereof, in an amount up to 100 percent of the difference between the market price and the option price. Options to purchase common stock under the 1991 Option Plan have been granted to Company employees at fair market value at the date of grant.

Our stock option plan (the 1999 Option Plan) was approved by share owners in April of 1999. Following the approval of the 1999 Option Plan, no grants were made from the 1991 Option Plan and shares available under the 1991 Option Plan were no longer available to be granted. Under the 1999 Option Plan, a maximum of 120 million shares of our common stock was approved to be issued or transferred to certain officers and employees pursuant to stock options granted under the 1999 Option Plan. Options to purchase common stock under the 1999 Option Plan have been granted to Company employees at fair market value at the date of grant.

Generally, stock options become exercisable over a four-year vesting period and expire 15 years from the date of grant. Prior to 1999, generally, stock options became exercisable over a three-year vesting period and expired 10 years from the date of grant.

The fair value of each option grant is estimated on the date of grant using the Black-Scholes option-pricing model with the following weighted-average assumptions used for grants in 2000, 1999 and 1998, respectively: dividend yields of 1.2, 1.2 and 0.9 percent; expected volatility of 31.7, 27.1 and 24.1 percent; risk-free interest rates of 5.8, 6.2 and 4.0 percent; and expected lives of five years for 2000 and four years for 1999 and 1998. The weighted-average fair value of options granted was $19.85, $15.77 and $15.41 for the years ended December 31, 2000, 1999 and 1998, respectively.

59

Notes to Consolidated Financial Statements

The Coca-Cola Company and Subsidiaries

A summary of stock option activity under all plans is as follows (shares in millions):

| | 2000 | | 1999 | | 1998 | |
	Shares	Weighted-Average Exercise Price	Shares	Weighted-Average Exercise Price	Shares	Weighted-Average Exercise Price
Outstanding on January 1,	101	$ 46.66	80	$ 42.77	80	$ 33.22
Granted [1]	32	57.35	28	53.53	17	65.91
Exercised	(12)	26.00	(6)	26.12	(16)	18.93
Forfeited/Expired [2]	(9)	57.51	(1)	60.40	(1)	55.48
Outstanding on December 31,	112	$ 51.23	101	$ 46.66	80	$ 42.77
Exercisable on December 31,	60	$ 46.57	59	$ 39.40	52	$ 32.41
Shares available on December 31, for options that may be granted	65		92		18	

[1] No grants were made from the 1991 Option Plan during 1999 or 2000.

[2] Shares Forfeited/Expired relate to the 1991 and 1999 Option Plans.

The following table summarizes information about stock options at December 31, 2000 (shares in millions):

| | Outstanding Stock Options | | | Exercisable Stock Options | |
Range of Exercise Prices	Shares	Weighted-Average Remaining Contractual Life	Weighted-Average Exercise Price	Shares	Weighted-Average Exercise Price
$ 10.00 to $ 20.00	2	0.8 years	$ 15.37	2	$ 15.37
$ 20.01 to $ 30.00	11	3.1 years	$ 23.41	11	$ 23.41
$ 30.01 to $ 40.00	10	4.8 years	$ 35.63	10	$ 35.63
$ 40.01 to $ 50.00	10	5.8 years	$ 48.86	9	$ 48.86
$ 50.01 to $ 60.00	65	8.9 years	$ 56.31	17	$ 57.06
$ 60.01 to $ 86.75	14	7.8 years	$ 65.87	11	$ 65.90
$ 10.00 to $ 86.75	112	7.4 years	$ 51.23	60	$ 46.57

NOTE 13: PENSION AND OTHER POSTRETIREMENT BENEFIT PLANS

Our Company sponsors and/or contributes to pension and postretirement health care and life insurance benefit plans covering substantially all U.S. employees and certain employees in international locations. We also sponsor nonqualified, unfunded defined benefit pension plans for certain officers and other employees. In addition, our Company and its subsidiaries have various pension plans and other forms of postretirement arrangements outside the United States.

Total expense for all benefit plans, including defined benefit pension plans, defined contribution pension plans, and postretirement health care and life insurance benefit plans, amounted to approximately $116 million in 2000, $108 million in 1999 and $119 million in 1998. In addition, the Company recorded a charge of $124 million for special retirement benefits as part of the Realignment discussed in Note 16. Net periodic cost for our pension and other benefit plans consists of the following (in millions):

| Year Ended December 31, | Pension Benefits | | |
	2000	1999	1998
Service cost	$ 54	$ 67	$ 56
Interest cost	119	111	105
Expected return on plan assets	(132)	(119)	(105)
Amortization of prior service cost	4	6	3
Recognized net actuarial (gain) loss	(7)	7	9
Settlements and curtailments	1	—	—
Net periodic pension cost	$ 39	$ 72	$ 68

| Year Ended December 31, | Other Benefits | | |
	2000	1999	1998
Service cost	$ 12	$ 14	$ 14
Interest cost	29	22	25
Expected return on plan assets	(1)	(1)	(1)
Amortization of prior service cost	1	—	—
Recognized net actuarial (gain) loss	(1)	—	—
Net periodic cost	$ 40	$ 35	$ 38

60

Notes to Consolidated Financial Statements

The Coca-Cola Company and Subsidiaries

The following table sets forth the change in benefit obligation for our benefit plans (in millions):

December 31,	Pension Benefits		Other Benefits	
	2000	1999	2000	1999
Benefit obligation at beginning of year	$1,670	$1,717	$303	$381
Service cost	54	67	12	14
Interest cost	119	111	29	22
Foreign currency exchange rate changes	(55)	(13)	—	—
Amendments	57	4	21	—
Actuarial (gain) loss	77	(137)	25	(101)
Benefits paid	(146)	(84)	(17)	(14)
Settlements and curtailments	(67)	—	13	—
Special retirement benefits	104	—	20	—
Other	6	5	1	1
Benefit obligation at end of year	$1,819	$1,670	$407	$303

The following table sets forth the change in plan assets for our benefit plans (in millions):

December 31,	Pension Benefits		Other Benefits	
	2000	1999	2000	1999
Fair value of plan assets at beginning of year [1]	$1,722	$1,516	$29	$36
Actual return on plan assets	4	259	2	1
Employer contribution	31	34	—	5
Foreign currency exchange rate changes	(57)	(20)	—	—
Benefits paid	(120)	(69)	(14)	(14)
Settlements	(38)	—	—	—
Other	13	2	—	1
Fair value of plan assets at end of year [1]	$1,555	$1,722	$17	$29

[1] Pension benefit plan assets primarily consist of listed stocks including 1,621,050 and 1,584,000 shares of common stock of our Company with a fair value of $99 million and $92 million as of December 31, 2000 and 1999, respectively.

The projected benefit obligation, accumulated benefit obligation and fair value of plan assets for the pension plans with benefit obligations in excess of plan assets were $570 million, $480 million and $152 million, respectively, as of December 31, 2000, and $556 million, $434 million and $161 million, respectively, as of December 31, 1999.

The accrued pension and other benefit costs recognized in our accompanying Consolidated Balance Sheets are computed as follows (in millions):

December 31,	Pension Benefits		Other Benefits	
	2000	1999	2000	1999
Funded status	$(264)	$52	$(390)	$(274)
Unrecognized net (asset) liability at transition	(6)	4	—	—
Unrecognized prior service cost	90	54	23	4
Unrecognized net gain	(89)	(285)	(51)	(91)
Net liability recognized	$(269)	$(175)	$(418)	$(361)
Prepaid benefit cost	$39	$73	$—	$—
Accrued benefit liability	(374)	(305)	(418)	(361)
Accumulated other comprehensive income	43	26	—	—
Intangible asset	23	31	—	—
Net liability recognized	$(269)	$(175)	$(418)	$(361)

The weighted-average assumptions used in computing the preceding information are as follows:

December 31,	Pension Benefits		
	2000	1999	1998
Discount rate	7%	7%	6 1/2%
Rate of increase in compensation levels	4 1/2%	4 1/2%	4 1/2%
Expected long-term rate of return on plan assets	8 1/2%	8 1/2%	8 3/4%

December 31,	Other Benefits		
	2000	1999	1998
Discount rate	7 1/2%	8%	6 3/4%
Rate of increase in compensation levels	4 3/4%	5%	4 1/2%
Expected long-term rate of return on plan assets	3%	3%	3%

The rate of increase in per capita costs of covered health care benefits is assumed to be 7 percent in 2001, decreasing gradually to 5 1/4 percent by the year 2005.

61

Notes to Consolidated Financial Statements
The Coca-Cola Company and Subsidiaries

A one percentage point change in the assumed health care cost trend rate would have the following effects (in millions):

	One Percentage Point Increase	One Percentage Point Decrease
Effect on accumulated postretirement benefit obligation as of December 31, 2000	$ 55	$ (45)
Effect on net periodic postretirement benefit cost in 2000	$ 8	$ (6)

NOTE 14: INCOME TAXES

Income before income taxes consists of the following (in millions):

Year Ended December 31,	2000	1999	1998
United States	$ 1,497	$ 1,504	$ 1,979
International	1,902	2,315	3,219
	$ 3,399	$ 3,819	$ 5,198

Income tax expense (benefit) consists of the following (in millions):

Year Ended December 31,	United States	State & Local	International	Total
2000				
Current	$ 48	$ 16	$ 1,155	$ 1,219
Deferred	(9)	46	(34)	3
1999				
Current	$ 395	$ 67	$ 829	$ 1,291
Deferred	182	11	(96)	97
1998				
Current	$ 683	$ 91	$ 929	$ 1,703
Deferred	(73)	28	7	(38)

We made income tax payments of approximately $1,327 million, $1,404 million and $1,559 million in 2000, 1999 and 1998, respectively. During the first quarter of 2000, the United States and Japan taxing authorities entered into an Advance Pricing Agreement (APA) whereby the level of royalties paid by Coca-Cola (Japan) Company, Ltd. (our Subsidiary) to our Company has been established for the years 1993 through 2001. Pursuant to the terms of the APA, our Subsidiary has filed amended returns for the applicable periods reflecting the negotiated royalty rate. These amended returns resulted in the payment during the first and second quarters of 2000 of additional Japanese taxes, the effect of which on both our financial performance and our effective tax rate was not material, due primarily to offsetting tax credits on our U.S. income tax return.

A reconciliation of the statutory U.S. federal rate and effective rates is as follows:

Year Ended December 31,	2000	1999	1998
Statutory U.S. federal rate	35.0 %	35.0 %	35.0%
State income taxes-net of federal benefit	.8	1.0	1.0
Earnings in jurisdictions taxed at rates different from the statutory U.S. federal rate	(4.0)	(6.0)	(4.3)
Equity income or loss [1]	2.9	1.6	—
Other operating charges [2]	1.9	5.3	—
Other-net	(.6)	(.6)	.3
	36.0 %	36.3 %	32.0%

[1] Includes charges by equity investees. See Note 15.

[2] Includes charges related to certain bottling, manufacturing and intangible assets. See Note 15.

Our effective tax rate reflects the tax benefit derived from having significant operations outside the United States that are taxed at rates lower than the U.S. statutory rate of 35 percent.

In 2000, management concluded that it was more likely than not that local tax benefits would not be realized with respect to principally all of the items discussed in Note 15, with the exception of approximately $188 million of charges related to the settlement terms of a class action discrimination lawsuit. Accordingly, valuation allowances were recorded to offset the future tax benefit of these nonrecurring items resulting in an increase in our effective tax rate. Excluding the impact of these nonrecurring items, the effective tax rate on operations for the year was slightly more than 30 percent.

In 1999, the Company recorded a charge of $813 million, primarily reflecting the impairment of certain bottling, manufacturing and intangible assets. For some locations with impaired assets, management concluded that it was more likely than not that no local tax benefit would be realized. Accordingly, a valuation allowance was recorded offsetting the future tax benefits for such locations. This resulted in an increase in our effective tax rate for 1999. Excluding the impact, the Company's effective tax rate for 1999 would have been 31.0 percent.

We have provided appropriate U.S. and international taxes for earnings of subsidiary companies that are expected to be remitted to the parent company. Exclusive of amounts that would result in little or no tax if remitted, the cumulative amount of unremitted earnings from our international subsidiaries that is expected to be indefinitely reinvested was approximately $3.7 billion on December 31, 2000. The taxes that would be paid upon remittance of these indefinitely reinvested earnings are approximately $1.3 billion, based on current tax laws.

62

Notes to Consolidated Financial Statements

The Coca-Cola Company and Subsidiaries

The tax effects of temporary differences and carryforwards that give rise to deferred tax assets and liabilities consist of the following (in millions):

December 31,	2000	1999
Deferred tax assets:		
Benefit plans	$ 261	$ 311
Liabilities and reserves	456	169
Net operating loss carryforwards	375	196
Other operating charges	321	254
Other	126	272
Gross deferred tax assets	1,539	1,202
Valuation allowance	(641)	(443)
	$ 898	$ 759
Deferred tax liabilities:		
Property, plant and equipment	$ 425	$ 320
Equity investments	228	397
Intangible assets	224	197
Other	129	99
	$ 1,006	$ 1,013
Net deferred tax asset (liability)[1]	$ (108)	$ (254)

[1] Deferred tax assets of $250 million and $244 million have been included in the consolidated balance sheet caption "Marketable securities and other assets" at December 31, 2000 and 1999, respectively.

On December 31, 2000 and 1999, we had approximately $143 million and $233 million, respectively, of gross deferred tax assets, net of valuation allowances, located in countries outside the United States.

On December 31, 2000, we had $968 million of operating loss carryforwards available to reduce future taxable income of certain international subsidiaries. Loss carryforwards of $635 million must be utilized within the next five years; $333 million can be utilized over an indefinite period. A valuation allowance has been provided for a portion of the deferred tax assets related to these loss carryforwards.

NOTE 15: NONRECURRING ITEMS

In the first quarter of 2000, we recorded charges of approximately $405 million related to the impairment of certain bottling, manufacturing and intangible assets, primarily within our Indian bottling operations. These impairment charges were recorded to reduce the carrying value of the identified assets to fair value. Fair value was derived using cash flow analysis. The assumptions used in the cash flow analysis were consistent with those used in our internal planning process. The assumptions included estimates of future growth in unit cases, estimates of gross margins, estimates of the impact of exchange rates and estimates of tax rates and tax incentives. The charge was primarily the result of our revised outlook for the Indian beverage market including the future expected tax environment. The remaining carrying value of long-lived assets

within our Indian bottling operations, immediately after recording the impairment charge, was approximately $300 million.

In the third quarter of 2000, we recorded a gain related to the merger of Coca-Cola Beverages and Hellenic Bottling Company. This merger resulted in a decrease of our Company's equity ownership interest from approximately 50.5 percent of Coca-Cola Beverages to approximately 24 percent of the combined entity, CCHBC. As a result of our Company's decreased equity ownership, a tax-free noncash gain of approximately $118 million was recognized.

In the fourth quarter of 2000, we recorded charges of approximately $188 million related to the settlement terms of, and direct costs related to, a class action discrimination lawsuit. The monetary settlement includes cash payments to fund back pay, compensatory damages, a promotional achievement fund and attorneys' fees. In addition, the Company introduced a wide range of training, monitoring and mentoring programs. Of the $188 million, $50 million was donated to The Coca-Cola Foundation to continue its broad range of community support programs. Under the terms of the settlement agreement, the Company has the option to rescind the agreement if more than 200 potential class members opt out of the settlement.

In 2000, the Company also recorded a nonrecurring charge of approximately $306 million, which represents the Company's portion of a charge recorded by Coca-Cola Amatil to reduce the carrying value of its investment in the Philippines. In addition, Panamco wrote down selected assets, including the impairment of the value of its Venezuelan operating unit. The Company's portion of this charge was approximately $124 million. Also contributing to the equity losses were nonrecurring charges recorded by investees in Eurasia and the Middle East. These nonrecurring charges were partially offset by the impact of lower tax rates related to current and deferred taxes at CCEAG.

In the fourth quarter of 1999, we recorded charges of approximately $813 million. Of this $813 million, approximately $543 million related to the impairment of certain bottling, manufacturing and intangible assets, primarily within our Russian and Caribbean bottlers and in the Middle and Far East and in North America. These impairment charges were recorded to reduce the carrying value of the identified assets to fair value. Fair values were derived using a variety of methodologies, including cash flow analysis, estimates of sales proceeds and independent appraisals. Where cash flow analyses were used to estimate fair values, key assumptions employed, consistent with those used in our internal planning process included our estimates of future growth in unit case sales, estimates of gross margins and estimates of the impact of inflation and foreign currency fluctuations. The charges were primarily the result of our revised outlook in certain markets due to the prolonged severe economic downturns. The remaining carrying value of these impaired long-lived assets, immediately after recording the impairment charge, was approximately $140 million.

63

Notes to Consolidated Financial Statements
The Coca-Cola Company and Subsidiaries

Of the $813 million, approximately $196 million related to charges associated with the impairment of the distribution and bottling assets of our vending operations in Japan and our bottling operations in the Baltics. The charges reduced the carrying value of these assets to their fair value less the cost to sell. Consistent with our long-term bottling investment strategy, management has committed to a plan to sell our ownership interest in these operations to one of our strategic business partners. The remaining carrying value of long-lived assets within these operations and the income from operations on an after-tax basis as of and for the 12-month period ending December 31, 2000, were approximately $143 million and $21 million, respectively.

On December 22, 2000, the Company signed a definitive agreement to sell the assets of our vending operations in Japan. The expected proceeds from the sale of the assets are equal to the current carrying value of the long-lived assets less the cost to sell. The sale transaction is expected to close in early 2001.

Management had intended to sell the assets of our bottling operations in the Baltics to one of our strategic business partners. That partner is currently in the process of an internal restructuring and no longer plans to purchase the Baltics bottling operations. At this time another suitable buyer has not been identified. Therefore, the Company will continue to operate the Baltics bottlers as consolidated operations until a new buyer is identified.

The remainder of the $813 million charges, approximately $74 million, primarily related to the change in senior management and charges related to organizational changes within the Europe and Eurasia, Latin America and Corporate segments. These charges were incurred during the fourth quarter of 1999.

In the second quarter of 1998, we recorded a nonrecurring charge primarily related to the impairment of certain assets in North America of $25 million and Corporate of $48 million.

NOTE 16: REALIGNMENT COSTS

In January 2000, our Company initiated a major organizational Realignment intended to put more responsibility, accountability and resources in the hands of local business units of the Company so as to fully leverage the local capabilities of our system.

Under the Realignment, employees were separated from almost all functional areas of the Company's operations, and certain activities have been outsourced to third parties. The total number of employees separated as of December 31, 2000, was approximately 5,200. Employees separated from the Company as a result of the Realignment were offered severance or early retirement packages, as appropriate, which included both financial and nonfinancial components. The Realignment expenses included costs associated with involuntary terminations, voluntary retirements and other direct costs associated with implementing the Realignment. Other direct costs included repatriating and relocating employees to local markets; asset write-downs; lease cancellation costs; and costs associated with the development, communication and administration of the Realignment.

The table below summarizes accrued Realignment expenses and amounts charged against the accrual as of and for the year ended December 31, 2000 (in millions):

Realignment Summary	Expenses	Payments	Noncash and Exchange	Accrued Balance December 31
Employees involuntarily separated				
Severance pay and benefits	$ 216	$ (123)	$ (2)	$ 91
Outside services — legal, outplacement, consulting	33	(25)	—	8
Other — including asset write-downs	81	(37)	(7)	37
	$ 330	$ (185)	$ (9)	$ 136
Employees voluntarily separated				
Special retirement pay and benefits	$ 353	$ (174)	$ —	$ 179
Outside services — legal, outplacement, consulting	6	(3)	—	3
	$ 359	$ (177)	$ —	$ 182
Other direct costs	$ 161	$ (92)	$ (9)	$ 60
Total Realignment	$ 850	$ (454)	$ (18)	$ 378[1]

[1] Accrued realignment expenses of approximately $254 million and $124 million have been included in the consolidated balance sheet captions "Accounts payable and accrued expenses" and "Other liabilities," respectively.

64

Notes to Consolidated Financial Statements

The Coca-Cola Company and Subsidiaries

NOTE 17: ACQUISITIONS AND INVESTMENTS

In separate transactions during the first half of 2000, our Company purchased two bottlers in Brazil, Companhia Mineira de Refrescos, S.A., and Refrigerantes Minas Gerais Ltda. In October 2000, the Company purchased a 58 percent interest in Paresa, a bottler located in Paraguay. In December 2000, the Company made a tender offer for the remaining 42 percent of the shares in Paresa. In January 2001, we completed the tender offer. We currently own approximately 95 percent of Paresa. During 2000, our Company's acquisition and investment activity totaled approximately $400 million.

During 1999, the Company's acquisition and investment activity, which included the acquisition of beverage brands from Cadbury Schweppes plc and investments in the bottling operations of Coca-Cola Embonor S.A., F&N Coca-Cola, and Coca-Cola West Japan Company, Ltd., totaled $1.9 billion. During 1998, the Company's acquisition and investment activity totaled $1.4 billion. None of the acquisitions and investment activity in 1998 was individually significant.

In July 1999, we completed the acquisition of Cadbury Schweppes plc beverage brands in 155 countries for approximately $700 million. These brands included Schweppes, Canada Dry, Dr Pepper, Crush and certain regional brands. Among the countries excluded from this transaction were the United States, South Africa, Norway, Switzerland and the European Union member nations (other than the United Kingdom, Ireland and Greece). In September 1999, we completed the acquisition of Cadbury Schweppes beverage brands in New Zealand for approximately $20 million. Also in September 1999, in a separate transaction valued at approximately $250 million, we acquired the carbonated soft-drink business of Cadbury Schweppes (South Africa) Limited in South Africa, Botswana, Namibia, Lesotho and Swaziland.

The acquisitions and investments have been accounted for by either the purchase, equity or cost method of accounting, as appropriate. Their results have been included in the Consolidated Financial Statements from their respective dates of acquisition using the appropriate method of accounting. Had the results of these businesses been included in operations commencing with 1998, the reported results would not have been materially affected.

NOTE 18: OPERATING SEGMENTS

Effective January 1, 2000, two of our Company's operating segments were geographically reconfigured and renamed. The Middle East and North Africa Division was added to the Africa Group, which changed its name to the Africa and Middle East Group. At the same time the Middle and Far East Group, less the relocated Middle East and North Africa Division, changed its name to the Asia Pacific Group. In the fourth quarter of 2000, the Greater Europe Group was renamed the Europe and Eurasia Group. Prior period amounts have been reclassified to conform to the current period presentation.

Our Company's operating structure includes the following operating segments: the North America Group (including The Minute Maid Company); the Africa and Middle East Group; the Europe and Eurasia Group; the Latin America Group; the Asia Pacific Group; and Corporate. The North America Group includes the United States and Canada.

Segment Products and Services

The business of our Company is nonalcoholic ready-to-drink beverages, principally soft drinks, but also a variety of noncarbonated beverages. Our operating segments derive substantially all their revenues from the manufacture and sale of beverage concentrates and syrups with the exception of Corporate, which derives its revenues primarily from the licensing of our brands in connection with merchandise.

Method of Determining Segment Profit or Loss

Management evaluates the performance of its operating segments separately to individually monitor the different factors affecting financial performance. Segment profit or loss includes substantially all the segment's costs of production, distribution and administration. Our Company manages income taxes on a global basis. Thus, we evaluate segment performance based on profit or loss before income taxes, exclusive of any significant gains or losses on the disposition of investments or other assets. Our Company typically manages and evaluates equity investments and related income on a segment level. However, we manage certain significant investments, such as our equity interests in Coca-Cola Enterprises, at the Corporate segment. We manage financial costs, such as exchange gains and losses and interest income and expense, on a global basis at the Corporate segment.

65

Notes to Consolidated Financial Statements
The Coca-Cola Company and Subsidiaries

Information about our Company's operations by operating segment is as follows (in millions):

	North America	Africa & Middle East	Europe & Eurasia	Latin America	Asia Pacific	Corporate	Consolidated
2000							
Net operating revenues	$7,870	$729	$4,377	$2,174	$5,159[1]	$ 149	$20,458
Operating income[2]	1,406	80	1,415[3]	916	956	(1,082)[4]	3,691
Interest income						345	345
Interest expense						447	447
Equity income (loss)[5]	3	(73)	35	(75)	(290)	111	(289)
Identifiable operating assets	4,271	622	1,408	1,545	1,953	5,270[6]	15,069
Investments[7]	141	338	1,757	1,767	993	769	5,765
Capital expenditures	259	11	194	16	132	121	733
Depreciation and amortization	244	54	64	96	211	104	773
Income before income taxes	1,410	(6)	1,568[8]	866	651	(1,090)	3,399
1999							
Net operating revenues	$7,519	$792	$4,540	$1,961	$4,828[1]	$ 165	$19,805
Operating income[9]	1,436	67	1,068	840	1,194	(623)	3,982
Interest income						260	260
Interest expense						337	337
Equity income (loss)	(5)	(29)	(73)	(5)	(37)	(35)	(184)
Identifiable operating assets	3,591	672	1,624	1,653	2,439	4,852[6]	14,831
Investments[7]	139	333	1,870	1,833	1,837	780	6,792
Capital expenditures	269	22	218	67	317	176	1,069
Depreciation and amortization	263	47	80	96	184	122	792
Income before income taxes	1,432	24	984	846	1,143	(610)	3,819
1998							
Net operating revenues	$6,934	$780	$4,827	$2,240	$3,856[1]	$ 176	$18,813
Operating income	1,383[10]	223	1,655	1,056	1,343	(693)[10]	4,967
Interest income						219	219
Interest expense						277	277
Equity income (loss)	(1)	(21)	(47)	68	(38)	71	32
Identifiable operating assets	3,467	541	1,711	1,364	1,595	3,781[6]	12,459
Investments[7]	141	312	2,010	1,629	1,979	615	6,686
Capital expenditures	274	22	216	72	104	175	863
Depreciation and amortization	231	40	92	93	101	88	645
Income before income taxes	1,392	192	1,577	1,132	1,289	(384)	5,198

Intercompany transfers between operating segments are not material.
Certain prior year amounts have been reclassified to conform to the current year presentation.

[1] Japan revenues represent approximately 75 percent of total Asia Pacific operating segment revenues related to 2000, and 80 percent related to 1999 and 1998.
[2] Operating income was reduced by $3 million for North America, $397 million for Asia Pacific and $5 million for Corporate related to the other operating charges recorded for asset impairments in the first quarter of 2000. Operating income was also reduced by $128 million for North America, $64 million for Africa and Middle East, $174 million for Europe and Eurasia, $63 million for Latin America, $127 million for Asia Pacific and $294 million for Corporate as a result of other operating charges associated with the Realignment.
[3] Operating income was reduced by $30 million for Europe and Eurasia due to incremental marketing expenses in Central Europe.
[4] Operating income was reduced by $188 million for Corporate related to the settlement terms of a discrimination lawsuit and a donation to The Coca-Cola Foundation.
[5] Equity income (loss) was reduced by $9 million for Africa and Middle East, $26 million for Europe and Eurasia, $124 million for Latin America and $306 million for Asia Pacific, as a result of our Company's portion of nonrecurring charges recorded by equity investees.
[6] Corporate identifiable operating assets are composed principally of marketable securities, finance subsidiary receivables, goodwill and other intangible assets and fixed assets.
[7] Principally equity investments in bottling companies.
[8] Income before taxes was increased by $118 million for Europe and Eurasia as a result of a gain related to the merger of Coca-Cola Beverages plc and Hellenic Bottling Company S.A.
[9] Operating income was reduced by $34 million for North America, $79 million for Africa and Middle East, $430 million for Europe and Eurasia, $35 million for Latin America, $176 million for Asia Pacific and $59 million for Corporate related to the other operating charges recorded in the fourth quarter of 1999.
[10] Operating income was reduced by $25 million for North America and $48 million for Corporate for provisions related to the impairment of certain assets.

Compound Growth Rates Ending 2000	North America	Africa & Middle East	Europe & Eurasia	Latin America	Asia Pacific	Consolidated
Net operating revenues						
5 years	7.3%	.1 %	(6.1)%	2.2 %	6.9%	2.4 %
10 years	6.4%	11.6 %	3.5 %	10.2 %	11.1%	7.1 %
Operating income						
5 years	10.6%	(19.4)%	.3 %	1.6 %	(5.4)%	(1.7)%
10 years	11.4%	(3.0)%	6.1 %	11.9 %	4.2 %	6.6 %